THE PROPERTY MILLIONAIRE METHOD

THE AUTHENTIC WAY TO TURN YOUR NEST EGG INTO MILLIONS, IN ANY MARKET

LORRAINE GANNON
AND RICK GANNON

Published by Known Publishing, 2022.

Paperback 978-1-915850-04-1
Ebook 978-1-915850-05-8

KNOWN

www.get-known.co.uk

WILL YOU BE ONE OF THE 25 MILLION NEW MILLIONAIRES IN THE WORLD IN 2025?

Despite the worldwide downturn since the Covid-19 pandemic, experts in wealth generation are expecting there to be a huge increase in the creation of new millionaires in the next three years.

In 2021, there were 62.5 million millionaires in the world. But that number is expected to jump 40% and reach 87.5 million over the next five years, according to Credit Suisse Group AG's Global Wealth Report 2022.[1]

Will you be one of those 25 million new millionaires?

This book gives you the choice to decide and take action; it is just one way you can increase your net worth by millions.

CONTENTS

PART TWO: MONEY

FOREWORD

Wow. This book isn't like most property books out there – it is loaded cover to cover with valuable content and goes far deeper than 99% of books out there. There's no fluff, just pure content. I'm not only talking property – this has also helped me to understand and refine my strategy, taking into account the wider economy, my personal investor profile and my goals. MASSIVE thanks to Rick and Lorraine for sharing so much here!

Sam Lawson, portfolio owner and property investor in Swindon, UK.

Sam was a student of ours about four years ago, and now he has a £4.91 million property portfolio. Sam specialises in using lease options, as a low-capital method to grow a large portfolio.

THE PROPERTY MILLIONAIRE METHOD™

If we said we could teach you how to take a small pot of money and become a property millionaire, in any market with property investing, and that the money doesn't have to be yours, then you would ask us how. And then tell us to prove it!

Our experience has proven this method works for us, for our mentees and our friends and family. You can make up your own mind about whether it will work for you. We know that you have to believe it is possible before you even try to become a property millionaire; if you don't believe you can do it, then your chances of making it happen are very low.

If you believe that you're not good enough to make it happen, you'll validate that belief and make it a reality and stay where you are. However, if you believe that you are good enough to make the Property Millionaire Method™ a reality, you will develop that property portfolio and who knows where you could be in one, five or ten years' time.

We have done this and created a multimillion-pound portfolio and realised millions of pounds of equity. Our lives are dramatically different from where we started. Rick was a police officer and Lorraine was running her own consultancy business; now we have a lifestyle that includes the freedom to work when we want, our dream home, a bungalow on the beach and holidays. We are extremely grateful for all that we have, and it is all thanks to property. We are now fulfilling our purpose to help others do the same.

This book will help you to believe you can do it too, in any market and with or without your own funds.

IT'S TOUGH BEING A MONEY CARETAKER!

If you have money – that is, five figures plus – then you will know the worry and concern that your cash isn't growing.

The responsibility weighs heavy.

Somehow the opportunity will be lost, and it will be your fault. Someone will take it away from you. Your money will shrink with inflation and get chipped away with small indiscriminate transactions. You will squander your opportunity, because you will choose the wrong investment, the wrong strategy. You trust property (unlike the crypto markets; like us, you might know someone who has had £300,000 taken out of their wallet!). You trust property but just don't get how other people seem to grow to 20-plus properties when you only have a deposit for one, maybe half a property. If you have a nest egg, savings, a good income, equity in your home, an SSAS pension, an inheritance or redundancy, you will want to hang on to the funds and invest and grow them.

However, most people do one thing. They leave it in the bank, terrified they will make a mistake, never realising that having savings in the bank is like holding on to ice cubes in your hand in the Sahara Desert; no matter what you do, the ice melts. In the bank, your savings are being melted by inflation. In fact, if you invested in any property rather than leave the money in the bank, you'd make money in the long term. Over time, due to high demand, property increases in value and stays in line with inflation, not least because to build a new house requires labour and materials, both of which are impacted by increasing costs and, when you add the limited availability of land, while property goes through a boom and crash cycle, the underlying trend is up! In later chapters, we will show you how UK property values have doubled on average every decade in the last 70 years. Property is like the freezer in the Sahara Desert keeping your savings protected against inflation.

We know a colleague who had a lump sum, in the region of £500,000, and he sat with the money in the bank (just to be clear: details have been changed to protect their identity). The money was used for holidays, living expenses and shopping. It took about 10 years to disappear. Gone. If all he had done was buy five small cheap houses outright for £100,000, those houses would be worth double that now and he'd have £1,000,000 and rental income. We know the area well, and what saddens us is the loss and waste.

We learnt a similar lesson when we were thrown some money by the Bank of Scotland in 2005. Money was in free-flow at the time – the banks had extended lending and were offering it out everywhere. Our bank manager phoned us and offered us £80,000. We took it and bought a blue Audi cabriolet and a number plate, paid off our credit cards and took a few holidays. Gone.

The biggest risk in savings is not working your savings. Apathy is the enemy.

Most people would speculate that property investors make money and are wealthy. Very few people learn the method of how to scale and grow a property portfolio without huge sums of money. Most people start to look at property investing when their savings reach a level where they become uncomfortable with the fact that their money is eroding away with inflation and not working very hard for them, or they come into a sum of money – a divorce settlement, a parent's home they sell, an inheritance or redundancy.

Most people's experience of investing in property is buying their own home. Buying your own home is not creating income-generating assets that will make you wealthy. Most people buy their forever home and plan to die in it, never realising any income or releasing any capital from it. If you own your own home and it is worth £1 million but you plan to live there for the rest of your life, then that is not a million pounds you can spend. It's locked into your home.

The Property Millionaire Method is about creating income and wealth from properties that you rent out: somebody else pays you to live there, creating you monthly income and long-term wealth.

Some people who have picked up this book have bought and done up a property. They have made a few thousand but had to sell the property to realise the equity. They don't understand how to grow and scale a property portfolio that pays them each and every month.

Our lives before property investing were to get a career, specialise, become experts, before becoming handcuffed to a salary and role and unemployable in other jobs. That took all our headspace, time and energy, dodging burnout and hanging on in there until we could collect our pension.

'Surely there must be another way?' was the question we asked ourselves.

This book shows you the method that works in any market as long as you invest for the long term and are patient.

This book is about much more than just investing in property. It's about transforming your life through property investing.

It will give you choices and freedom, allowing you to realise your ambitions while making your dreams possible and giving you the opportunity to choose how you live your life.

The solution: it's about owning one million pounds' worth of property – property you don't live in – and then realising one million pounds' worth of wealth.

A DIFFERENT MODEL

This method is a financial paradigm shift.

And if you've never heard of the word paradigm (pronounced para-dime) before, this means a shift in the model, a break from the pattern.

Could you afford to retire now? Could you pay off your home and have enough income to afford to live?

In theory, the official retirement age is 67 in the UK (and similar in other countries) or week number 3,484 of your life.

The average life expectancy in the UK is 81.25 years,[2] which is about 741 weeks of retirement. To put it another way, 82% of your life will be gone by the time you are retiring, leaving only 18% of it for you to live in freedom, not having to earn a living. But will you have enough money to retire and live the lifestyle of your choice?

If you want to spend a lot of money and retire early doing the stuff you want with your life, then you need a plan. Starting this method today will make it much easier to realise than starting one year before you retire.

Property is not a 'get rich quick' opportunity. You might be disappointed by that, but hang on a minute... we honestly believe property is a 'get rich slow' opportunity. However, you can quickly set yourself up to do this. You could get a million pounds' worth of property in the next 12 months. That property could earn you money immediately and give you your income and replace your job.

You will need to choose carefully and wisely. You'd then need to wait for property prices to go up to create wealth.

As you will learn from this book, you partner with time when you invest in property.

Time and health are finite. These two things are the only variables that you need to successfully invest in property.

We are all capable of making money but the amount of money that arrives in a time period determines whether it is a relatively large or a small amount of money; £100,000 per hour and £100,000 per annum are very different. Time is very important when it comes to how money arrives in your bank account.

The timing of money is as important as the amount.

Most people are now capable of making £1 million in their careers. If your career is from ages 20 to 65 – 45 years – and you earn just over £22,000 per year, you will create a million pounds of earnings. Then tax is deducted. Then you have to pay your rent and mortgage and buy food.

Change the time frame of earning a million pounds to five years and you make £200,000 per year, then you will make a million pounds much quicker. You would still have to pay all the tax, rent, mortgage and food bills. But the £200k role and job would feel very different financially.

How much money you save and don't spend could help you buy property much more quickly, but that will very much depend on what stuff, experiences, freedoms or time you spend your cash on.

How you spend money, or whether you save money, will very much depend on your upbringing, your current circumstances and what you value.

What if you can't make £200k per annum?

How do you escape the time-for-money trap?

You have to find another way to make money, one that isn't based on your time or your earning ability.

In our opinion, property is a 'get rich slow' opportunity, particularly when you start out. But it quickly compounds after the first few years, and you get faster and faster growth in wealth.

This book is here to help you discover the Property Millionaire Method and it answers that question that keeps rattling around in your head:

Just how do other people do it?

'It' being the purchase of 10, 20, 30 or 40 properties. How do they get enough money to do it?

Well, the answer is they don't get lots and lots of deposits, they don't secretly print money or steal it; they have another secret. And it's really rather simple, although it requires focus, tenacity and resilience.

We don't want you to think of this book as some kind of scam. It's a process that we have discovered.

We've purchased many a training course, but nobody really explained it like this book will.

In fact, when we first started, we ended up owing our angel investors about £300,000 in just one year after we aggressively grew our portfolio. We fell into the investor trap. We borrowed funds that were tied up in the properties. We didn't have a way to repay the capital.

We did eventually. We did it through bloomin' hard work, making it happen. We borrowed more funds for a while, until the penny dropped, then we created such profitable deals that we repaid everyone.

Investors, or family and friends who lend you money, want a return 'of' their capital more than they want a return 'on' their capital.

Your income and wealth will be significantly increased through property investing if you follow the principles and methods of the Property Millionaire Method.

Most property investors, and beginners who are looking to grow a property portfolio, face one major hidden obstacle that keeps their dream just out of reach.

What is the obstacle?

Well, before we tell you, let's ask you a question...

The fact that you opened this book means that you're looking to change your life, yes?

Do you think owning £1 million of property will change your life in 10 years' time?

Do any of the following sound familiar?

1. **You've been in love with property for 10 years but still don't own much, and not much has happened.**

2. **You just can't work it out, you don't know how others get to 40-plus properties.**

3. **Nothing is sticking, no deals, no finance, no offers accepted, no plan...**

We're going to show you how to grow your portfolio to 40-plus properties. You can stop at 4, 10, 20 or 30, but this process is scalable.

Once you have read this book, you'll begin to realise how you can do it too.

Clarity is the key.

This book was designed to be read in an afternoon. Our vision is that you will spend a few hours reading it and then you will have a moment where you want to throw the book up in the air in excitement, when you suddenly 'get' this method and want to dance about like a silly person.

We want you to have your own lightbulb moments, penny-dropping stuff and any other 'inspiring moment' clichés. They will mean that you understand, you can believe this can happen for you too and you can go out there and do it.

For some people you might need to process this method for a few days and then suddenly, when you're just stepping out of the shower, there it will be. You will understand.

It's frustrating this stuff isn't taught in schools. That our parents and networks don't know this stuff. We believe we should be grateful for our education system. However, while not everyone can be a property investor, society couldn't function without the many roles needed.

Property is the perfect way to help others. You get to benefit from the income and capital growth and the tenant gets a good-quality home.

We personally can't create all the rental homes and new housing society needs. But we can share our method to help others create them. If everyone we directly work with creates 4, 10, 20, 30 or 40 homes for tenants, then we aim to be part of a million-home building effort. If this book has an impact across the world and inspires others, then we could double or treble that number.

And before we start talking about the gobbling up of housing stock by private landlords, consider that banks and financial institutions in the UK are currently working on a vision of being the biggest property landlord. Why? Because they can see the opportunity to create income and put their cash to use. We're not sure banks will make great landlords, but we know you will.

Now, despite what you might think, private landlords are much more approachable and generally better landlords than corporate giants. Put simply, they care. And we care about our tenants and their homes.

CAN YOU DO THIS?

There are some nuances that mean not everything will apply if you are investing outside of the UK, but the general principle of the Property Millionaire Method works worldwide, with the *one proviso* that there is an economic centre where you are investing. What do we mean by an economic centre? We are talking city centres, built-up suburban areas, where there are jobs, factories and commerce. Wherever there is a flow of money, there will be a need for homes and, in fact, a big demand. Find your investment area by completing the exercise in The Property Millionaire Planner.

We should also, at this point, alert you to the fact that there is also risk in property investing. You could lose money, so take advice from your financial adviser and property professionals. This book is based on our experiences and what has worked for us and has been tested by our students. Great property investing takes great advice and great know-how. Get yourself a good power team of professionals who can help you.

Anyone who has bought a house in the last 10 years plus will have seen huge growth in their house value. This is when property investing becomes a reality and a real truth for the masses who own their own homes. But the challenge is that you live in your own home. You have to pay for it. Rented property is paid for by the tenants.

Accidental landlords and first-time property investors often enter the market to invest cash and get better returns than bank interest rates. Finding property an inflation-beating and return-smashing investment, they then catch the property-investing bug.

How do you grow a property portfolio of more than just one house without needing huge amounts of cash?

The truth is that it's an easily learnt process called the Property Millionaire Method.

This method will get you a million pounds' worth of property, without consuming large cash reserves or deposits, but effectively leveraging whatever cash you have, your inheritance and hard-earnt savings. Learn this method or take the risk that a few wrong purchases and mistakes could cost you the growth of your portfolio and wealth for years, if not decades. This method is your clear path to growing a scalable property business.

There are lots of cliches about property:

- **Don't wait to buy property; buy property and wait.**
- **They're not making any more land; buy land now.**
- **The best investment on Earth is earth.**

If you are really focused and have the right information and resources, it's possible to obtain a million-pound portfolio in a year. But it does take a lot of focus.

However, most important is to follow a process of creating added value in the properties you buy.

All businesses that create profit add value to the customer in a product, package or service, and property investing is no different. You must add value to your property.

Most amateur property investors and accidental landlords think that because they have bought their main residential home that they can therefore just switch to being a property investor.

They know how to buy a house, right?

Therefore, they can do this property investing thing? Um, no!

In the UK average house prices are around £250,000 (it is actually higher than this, but we've rounded down for simplicity). Most property investors can buy one or two houses; as buy-to-let property purchasers, they need 25% deposit to get a UK mortgage, which is £62,500, plus some costs for legal and mortgage fees. Most property investors can save up a deposit for one or two properties and then get stuck. They don't have cash or deposits to invest and continue, so there is no scale in their investing. They are stuck at their ability to save up quickly enough to buy the next property.

The aim of the Property Millionaire Method is to get you *four* houses and a million pounds' worth of property– ideally in a year. In each quarter you should be able to buy, lease or rent a property that means you can cashflow and make an income while controlling a million pounds' worth of property. The long-term goal is to create a million pounds' worth of equity in property, giving you a £1 million net worth. Depending on property prices, this could be in 10 years or could be longer. The more property you control and own, the quicker this will be.

Breaking the barrier and buying four or more houses for most investors requires them to apply a model that can scale. Four houses on average will roughly make for a portfolio worth more than a million pounds. Once an investor gets four houses, the ability of the business to grow to 40 houses and ten million pounds' worth of property is unlocked. This is now a property business, creating huge personal wealth.

SOUNDS EASY - WHERE'S THE CATCH?

Property investing is a little confusing; at times it's easy and at times it's hard. You can use this method in any market conditions, and you don't always need your own money to do it.

There is one catch: your commitment to doing this, your ability to apply yourself and follow the recipe.

You must also be willing to be rejected loads and loads, and then some more.

Accept you will make mistakes but learn from them.

You commit to the process and principles of the Property Millionaire Method. This means you take weekly actions; you view properties, and you view the right properties for scaling, not just any old property. This is your viewing commitment.

You can use your pot of cash, or you can work with other people's money, such as investors, family or friends.

To scale, your ability to *recycle your funds* and pay back the money you borrowed is hugely important. This is your capital and cashflow foundations. Ignore this part of the Property Millionaire Method and you'll be in a whole heap of trouble, by either running out of money or not being able to pay back your investors. However, if you use the Property Millionaire Method then you will sleep soundly at night.

You will follow our eight-step INVESTOR Process™, which will lead you to acquire or control property. It's one thing to create a home, but you have to get tenants and guests to pay you. Legislation, licensing, planning, covenants, finance, charges, housing law, interior design, mortgage products, deal stacking, and health and safety all make property investing more involved than just buying the house. Follow the process to deal with all of these issues, so you are a compliant and legal property owner.

You will then repeat the process in quarterly sprints. You'll run four races/dashes per year, so you can get a million pounds' worth of property. Whether you are purchasing or using other property controlling tools, such as rent-to-rent or lease options (we'll discuss these tools later), focus on value creation.

Property investing is about detail, so ignore this at your peril. Details spring up even when you have done your due diligence and think you have it covered. At that moment it comes out of the woodwork to slap you on the chops. It can be tough at times, and you want to give up, but get stubborn, dig in and hold on because it's definitely worth it.

PART ONE

THE PROPERTY MILLIONAIRE METHOD™

CHAPTER 1

WHY DOES THE PROPERTY MILLIONAIRE METHOD™ WORK?

We know this is the bit you want, the juicy bit, so the aim is to tell you how and why this method works straight away, so you get clarity over the scalable process.

The goal is to get you four properties. At this milestone you are considered a professional landlord with the UK lending regulations. Plus, four properties add up to a million pounds of property value, based on current UK averages. The average value of a UK house in November 2022 was £292,598, according to the Halifax House Price Index,[3] but from here on in the book we round the average property price down to £250,000 because we are not looking to buy above the average house value. We are looking for the value-driven properties to add to our portfolios.

Historically, property prices have doubled in the UK on average every 10 years. Past performance isn't a guarantee of future performance, and in time, percentage growth and timescales could change. Recent world events and global pandemics have taught us all about how changeable the world is. Nothing can be taken for granted. Yet we have to live and work in this world. Therefore, we have to use what we can. History can be a great teacher, but we must be nimble and pivot when things change.

With a million pounds' worth of property in your ownership, when you partner with time, if the property doubles in value, your mortgage doesn't, and you will get yourself a million pounds of equity or net worth that is all yours. As long as you keep up the repayments on your mortgages (as your house could be repossessed if you don't), you will always own a million pounds' worth of property. We will discuss further the best ways to make sure you have plenty of income to do that too.

Compound interest works in our favour when we're investing. Inflation devalues our debt over time. In new house builds and developments, inflation can push the cost of property up with higher labour and material costs. House prices increase when supply is low and demand is high.

Let's discuss in more detail how you grow a portfolio of 10, 20, 30 or 40-plus properties.

Firstly, we need to understand the property market: the principles of why it is a strong market, what constraints are within the market. Think of this section as a bit of a 'strengths and weaknesses' interview question. If you are a property millionaire, you need to know how you are vulnerable and why you are strong. This builds up a confident or cautious approach and therefore a strong investing mindset.

WHAT PROPERTY MARKET INSIGHTS DO YOU NEED TO KNOW?

The UK property market has quite a lot of influences, some of which also apply in other areas of the world. The housing market is a complex system that is greatly influenced by a variety of factors.

One of the most fundamental factors that affects housing is need. Property is a need. We have a need to have shelter as human beings. Some businesses have a discretional service. You don't need all those kitchen gadgets; someone must 'sell' them to you. If you are at all like the Gannon household, you will have a kitchen full: we have a bread maker, a soup maker and a stock pot we don't use because we don't need it on a day-to-day basis. But because we have a family home and somewhere to live, we then spend our money on other discretional items, where the marketing and salespeople actively sell these items to us.

Most people actively go out and look to buy a property or rent a home. It's you who starts this search. Some services are a need, and property is one of them.

Abraham Maslow wrote a paper in 1943 called *A Theory of Human Motivation* in which he describes the stages of growth in humans.[4] Maslow used the terms below as *needs* to describe the pattern human motivations generally move through.

- **Physiological**
- **Safety**
- **Belongingness and love**
- **Esteem**
- **Self-actualisation**
- **Self-transcendence**

Our observations of these principles in practice came in March 2020, when the coronavirus shut down the UK and a sense of panic swept over the country.

We noticed that even our own motivations came back to how we keep putting food on the table (first priority) and then how we keep a roof over our heads (second priority).

Supermarkets experienced this in real time when dried pasta and tinned foods disappeared off the shelf. Lorraine remembers a moment in a supermarket where it was suddenly frowned upon to buy two fresh whole chickens, as people wanted equal distribution of food sources. It was crazy. Every household across the country also had the largest stock of toilet rolls they'd ever had. Cupboards and shelves were full of toilet tissue. It even started a craze on TikTok, and people started building 'walls' out of toilet rolls!

In Maslow's paper, he subsequently extends the idea to include his observations of humans' innate curiosity. We are all curious beings, and we are often curious about what we see others doing.

So, what does this have to do with the Property Millionaire Method? People tend to behave in 'connection' with each other. If one of your friends moves house, you might look up their house purchase, and then you might find yourself looking to move house too. It starts off a chain reaction. People behave and move in droves, and we can develop a herd mentality. If you are surrounded by friends and family who invest in property, then you are more likely to observe and copy this action.

As a property millionaire in the making, your role is to observe what the general trends are, what people are doing, what is changing in society. A chain reaction is started by one or two people moving and then their friends and family are also looking to move. Population confidence is established: 'if it's alright for them, then it's alright for me.'

If we look at how many people moved during the pandemic, in the 12 months to June 2021, 461,010 transactions took place, up by 50%, according to the *Evening Standard*.[5]

Over time, people's lifestyles change and this can affect the type of properties they want to buy or rent. Since the pandemic, people have been moving away from expensive areas around London and moving to areas where they can double the size of their home for no more investment. People have been looking for space, outdoor garden space and a home office, now that they can work from home.

Think about the trends: why are people moving home? What do they want? What type of lifestyle do they seek?

HOUSING ECONOMIC FACTORS: WHAT IS OUTSIDE OF YOUR CONTROL?

There are a whole host of factors that can affect the property market and are completely outside of your control.

Economic conditions

The health of the overall economy can have a big impact on the housing market. When people are confident about their job security and the overall economy, they are more likely to buy or rent a home. Conversely, when the economy is struggling, people are less likely to enter the housing market. During Covid, when the government supported wages and businesses, people had more cash, as they couldn't spend it; this then meant more people looked to move house, as they were more confident and their personal economy was good.

Interest rates

When interest rates are low, it is cheaper for people to borrow money to buy a home. This can lead to increased demand for housing, and higher prices. When interest rates are high, it is more expensive for people to borrow money, and more people rent homes rather than buying. People downscale when interest rates rise and are forced to move to more affordable homes, and this creates downward pressure on prices.

In the UK, the central Bank of England sets the base rate for interest. We have had over a decade of low-interest mortgages.

At the time of writing this book, even though interest rates have gone from 0.25 to 3%, mortgage interest rates are still relatively low (there are buy-to-let products at 5.69% for a five-year fix) compared with personal loans at 6–10%, credit cards at 18–30%, overdrafts at 12–25% and other consumer credit at 8–20%.

While all the other types of money we've just described buy things and fund your cost of living, buy-to-let mortgages fund an investment and the purchase of an asset – a purchase that could generate you an income and, in the long term, offer an increase in the property's value, giving you a substantial increase in your net worth.

The challenge with interest rates right now is not the relative percentage. The challenge is that property prices continue to grow, and low yields mean the property doesn't generate enough rent to pay for the interest. (The yield is the ability of the property to earn rent in relation to the overall property value.)

The UK average property yield is 3.7%,[6] which means your cost of money cannot be more than 3.7%. The property only earns 3.7% or 3.7p rent for every pound's worth of value of the property. It is the choice of property for the mortgage and not the relative percentage of the mortgage that will cause inexperienced and uneducated investors to make big mistakes and gain poor returns or even lose money when interest rates continue to increase. We will discuss this more later.

We have made mistakes and panicked when the potential for interest rates to increase has been 'talked up' in the press. We fixed at 7% for 10 years at a peak of interest rates in 2007. Interest rates quickly plummeted in the next few years, so while everyone was enjoying 0.5% interest rates, we had the joy of sitting out eight years at an extra 5–6% interest costs. Luckily, we had a high-cashflow property, so while it hurt, it wasn't disastrous.

No one holds a crystal ball to predict what will happen, but 10 years is a long time to fix for, and it was a big mistake off the back of our panicked view of the market. We would fix in at a cheap rate where we would see rates become value. The window of opportunity for fixing at cheap rates for 10 years plus has gone right now, due to the heat and attention in the market.

People's lives change; properties, industries and lifestyles change. Our view is to take a short- to medium-term approach to things. We tend to opt for five-year fixes on things now. This is long enough for economies to recover and the financial storms to pass, and it is reasonable for strategic business planning while covering short-term risk.

Taxes

Stamp Duty Land Tax (or SDLT) is charged by the UK government on property purchases in England and Northern Ireland (other taxes apply in Scotland and Wales). The amount charged can vary depending on the price of the home being purchased. During the pandemic the government offered incentives on SDLT to encourage people to get into the property market. The Chancellor of the Exchequer knows that an economy gets a boost whenever there is a strong housing market. Moving home triggers large amounts of spending from homeowners on decorating and furnishing their new homes. If low taxes trigger a market, then high taxes can suppress a market.

Similarly, the UK government introduced additional taxes for landlords on SDLT and on how they could claim back mortgage interest. This has led to many landlords exiting the market and retiring. There are more tax-efficient ways of setting up a property business, if you are starting out today, so speak to an accountant for the most effective approaches. It can be difficult for larger landlords to transfer into this new structure, and most don't or won't go through the hassle, so we are currently seeing lots of old-school landlords being crippled by the new tax rules and selling up.

Planning legislation

What you can build, alter, add and change about a property is subject to planning law; it is a complex system. Central government sets out central legislation and asks local councils to administer and enforce the law. It is a very emotive subject, as often there are many who do not want new homes, factories and offices built near them, but many people need housing, jobs and businesses. The planning system is complex, and more 'permitted development rights' have been introduced by central government to try to increase housing and give businesses more flexibility in regard to how they use commercial premises.

However, some planning permissions can take over 18 months to realise in preparation and consultation. It can be a prohibitively expensive and long process. We are great believers in the idea that wherever there are restrictions and a lack of flow, it can be difficult to create wealth at any pace. Money likes flow; it likes to move without friction.

Land and housing availability

There is a finite amount of land available in any given location. Developers are always looking for land to get permission to build new houses on and sometimes, when they have enough supply, they will 'land bank.' Developers want to enter a buoyant market and build when house prices are strong and demand is also very strong. If you are a large developer and building 100 houses, a price drop of 5% or more could significantly affect the return enough to postpone the building.

HOW TO DOUBLE YOUR MONEY PASSIVELY

As a general rule, if there is lots of demand from buyers but only a limited supply of homes to buy, prices will tend to be higher. In contrast, if there are more homes available than people looking for them, then vendors may have to reduce their prices in order to sell.

The worldwide population is scary; if you want to completely freak out then watch this algorithm of the population, showing that more babies are born than people die. The world is approaching a population of 8 billion people.[7]

In the book *The Future of Life,* Edward O. Wilson calculates the world's maximum population.[8] Wilson says, 'The constraints of the biosphere are fixed' and goes on to say that 'if everyone agreed to become vegetarian, leaving little or nothing for livestock, the present 1.4 billion hectares of arable land (3.5 billion acres) would support about 10 billion people.' So we are running out of resources as a population. All these people need somewhere to live, something to eat, places to go to school, to work and to farm. The world can only support so many people.

The UK population is growing at a fairly constant rate. This can create increased demand for housing because there are more people looking for homes to buy, rent and live in. It creates scarcity. A housing market can be affected by demographics, too. The baby boomers, who are now turning 70 years old, typically occupy large family homes with only one person or a couple living there, meaning there is less housing available for families. Prices of family homes are high because there are lots of large homes locked out of the market.

New property is built in order to meet a need or a want. When there is an increase in demand for property, it will lead to an increase in house prices.

Where there is strong demand, sellers are less likely to negotiate and drop their prices. This leads to property price inflation. However, when supply increases, property prices fall, which leads to deflation, and some people will find themselves in negative equity (the situation where the house is worth less than they paid for it).

Property prices increase due to supply and demand pressure, because we are not meeting supply and building enough new homes. The National Housing Federation and Crisis from Heriot-

“

New property is built in order to meet a need or a want. When there is an increase in demand for property, it will lead to an increase in house prices.

”

Watt University identified a need for 340,000 homes each year to 2031, of which 145,000 'must be affordable homes.'[9]

Interestingly, the government has a target of 300,000 new homes per year; this is already 40,000 below the target needed. In its report Tackling the Under-Supply of Housing (published in February 2022),[10] the government acknowledges the National Housing Federation and Crisis target of 340,000 but yet does not seek to fulfil it.

We currently do not have the infrastructure to cope with the housing crisis. Not enough new homes are being built, because we have a planning system that is breaking: planning officers are overworked and have too many applications coming in. The government cannot attract good planning officers, because they are paid far more by the private sector. The government acknowledges there is a consensus that we need to supply housing but recognises there is less consensus about how to actually deliver these needed homes.

This all points towards continued pressure on supply. We know that where supply is restricted, and because demand is so high, house prices look to continue to grow in the long term. Even if there are corrections in the market or house prices do fall a little, we predict long-term house prices are set to continue to rise.

Property price inflation was experienced during the property boom in the 80s and 90s. Property owners made a lot of money simply through ownership. The more you owned, the more you made.

The following table is a review of property prices over the last 70 years.[11]

YEAR	AVERAGE UK HOUSE PRICE
1950	£1,891
1960	£2,530
1970	£4,057
1980	£20,268
1990	£58,153
2000	£89,597
2010	£170,365
2020	£254,624

According to the Halifax House Price Index (November 2022), the current average UK property price is £292,598.

From 1950 to 2020, property prices doubled seven times:

- **£1,891 doubled = £3,782**
- **£3,782 doubled = £7,564**
- **£7,564 doubled = £15,128**
- **£15,128 doubled = £30,256**
- **£30,256 doubled = £60,512**
- **£60,512 doubled = £121,024**
- **£121,024 doubled = £242,048**

So that's seven doubles over 70 years, which means property prices double every 10 years *on average* – not every 10 years. There's a subtle but important distinction. We cannot guarantee, if you enter the property market today, that you will see the price of your property double on the ten-year anniversary.

Prices go up and down in the property market so, to keep the maths simple, we are going to use £250,000 to work through the following methods. Four houses with this benchmark should equate to £1 million of property.

THE BUY-TO-LET MARKET

Some would argue that this doubling of property prices doesn't take into account inflation and the increase in average wages, and that therefore the real effect is not a doubling of capital. There is definitely some merit to this when considering your own home and personal situation. Your own costs and overheads will also increase with inflation. Salaries may or may not increase to realise the extra equity. But in the buy-to-let market, the mortgage is effectively being paid for you by the rent you receive from your tenants, and so you are not having to earn a salary for inflation to be relevant to your earnings increasing or decreasing.

If you are using debt (i.e., a mortgage), then inflation actually helps devalue the relative level of debt. It's the ownership of an asset while your mortgage is being paid for by someone else. That's why it's such a powerful way to create wealth.

UK banks, and banks worldwide, like property as security for lending against. Imagine going to the bank and asking to borrow money to fund a purchase of bitcoin or stock shares.

'Yes, bank manager, that's right: I have £25,000 and I'd really like to borrow £75,000 so that I can leverage your money to buy more shares and bitcoin.'

Banks like houses and property because they are protected in the security of their asset and ownership by the UK system of HM Land Registry. Other countries may or may not have the same land registration system or legislation.

The HM Land Registry website says:[12]

'HM Land Registry safeguards land and property ownership valued at £7 trillion, enabling over £1 trillion worth of personal and commercial lending to be secured against property across England and Wales. The Land Register contains more than 26 million titles, showing evidence of ownership for more than 87% of the land mass of England and Wales.

Anyone buying or selling land or property, or taking out a mortgage, must apply to us to register:

- **Unregistered land or property**
- **Any new owner of registered land or property**
- **An interest affecting registered land or property, such as a mortgage, a lease or a right of way**

When considering each application, we use the law to decide whether and how it should be registered.

Register land or property with us, once land or property is entered in the register, we record any ownership changes, mortgages or leases that affect it. Anyone who suffers loss because of an error or omission in the register, or because the register needs to be corrected, will normally be compensated.

We are committed to carrying out our statutory and commercial business with fairness, openness, and honesty. We have policies and procedures to prevent bribery.'

This is why banks like property! It enables banks to lend at very low rates of interest, because a chartered surveyor indemnifies them against the valuation and HM Land Registry will compensate them if there is any error in ownership, mortgages or interests in the property. Their capital is protected. Their main risk is in your ability to pay the mortgage. If you are letting the property out, as long as you have a home to live in yourself (and therefore don't live there yourself), the risk for the bank is therefore actually in the tenants' ability to pay your rent and cover your mortgage.

RUNNING A PROPERTY PORTFOLIO VERSUS A BUSINESS

Sam Lawson was running a cruise ship entertainment agency before the pandemic. His business was seven figures and was well established. During lockdown the turnover went to zero. Luckily, Sam had the foresight to invest in property. He felt he had all of his eggs in one basket and that if anything happened to him, his business would stop. Sam started to invest in property two years before the pandemic started and was now realising £10k per month profit from his portfolio. He now has over 10 properties. This established a steady cashflow. Sam is now looking at investing in small developments, buying blocks of flats, a few houses and other strategies, now he has a secure baseline of cashflowing properties.

WHY IS THE ACCIDENTAL PROPERTY INVESTOR DESTINED TO REMAIN SMALL?

Old-school property investors and landlords used to buy a flat or a house, save up a deposit for the next one, and repeat. However, single-let investing is now not as scalable as it once was. As house prices climb, the amount of mortgage you can get is effectively limited by the monthly rental amount. This is the mortgage cover test. If you buy a property and do it up, you are limited to how much you can refinance if you now make the property worth more. This means that you can buy cheap and add value but you may be limited to the cash you can release for the next property by the refinance amount.

Most buy-to-let mortgages require a 25% deposit, so you are always limited by the deposit-building ability of your savings, business or other sources. We would not recommend you use borrowed or loaned funds from an investor, unless you are confident you can pay the investor back. Investors like great interest returns but they also like their capital returned. That's no joke – we've said this before, but it's so important for you to realise this that we are telling the editors to not delete this section, even though it's a duplication. Please understand the ramifications of borrowing money if you have no idea how you are going to pay it back.

We don't want you to remain small, which is why we have created the Property Millionaire Planner to accompany this book. The planner is designed to be the desktop companion for your property-investing journey, there to help you follow key processes, get the key activities completed and start filling in the portfolio pages with all the properties you buy, lease, manage and own. You may want to get a copy at www.newerapropertytraining.co.uk/planner.

SUMMARY

You can't get into property investing with the mindset that you know how to buy your own house and therefore you can buy an investment property. This mindset will get you stuck after your first purchase. You can't scale to a property portfolio of 10, 20, 30 or more houses without designing the business the correct way. It won't happen by accident or with a bit of luck.

You might buy a house, flip it on (industry term for selling it) and make a few thousand pounds. We are not dismissing this idea; buying and selling houses is actually a process that many start, learning a great deal about property investing along the way. Be warned, though: most people have never heard of the Construction and Design Management (CDM) regulations (2015), and they risk fines or imprisonment if an accident occurs and anyone is hurt or, God forbid, dies on site.

The UK Health and Safety Executive says:[13] 'For offences committed on and after 12th March 2015 the maximum penalty in the magistrates' court is an unlimited fine or imprisonment for a term not exceeding six months or both. In the Crown Court, the maximum penalty is an unlimited fine or imprisonment not exceeding two years or both.'

There are some fairly easy processes that you can implement to protect yourself and your building team. You are running a business and making profit. You are required to comply with legislation. None of this is hard once you are educated, but realising that you don't know how to do this yet is the key to making sure you are compliant with the law and that you design a business that is scalable and is not illegal.

It's entirely possible to grow and scale to 40-plus properties, all of them cashflowing you £500 per month profit. That's £20,000 per month. It won't be easy to do, but the process is simple enough.

The accidental investor is destined to remain small. Perhaps you have been left an inheritance, and while this might secure you one or two properties, it's not possible to accidentally scale to 10, 20, 30 or 40 properties. One or two houses are easy enough to acquire but go past four houses and then you need to take it seriously. The opportunity is here for the taking.

CHAPTER 2

HOW DOES THE PROPERTY MILLIONAIRE METHOD™ WORK?

In 1997 we couldn't sell our house. Rick had got a promotion and we bought a brand new four-bedroom house in Nottingham. We then decided to buy a pub, a big old building that we still own today; we bought a lease for only £15,000 and used some borrowed funds. We needed a solution for our house quickly, but a sale would have realised a £10,000 loss. Any new house purchase includes the developer's profit in the price; once 'used', a brand new house will take a while to recover the premium price that was charged because it was brand new.

We became buy-to-let landlords but didn't buy to make cashflow. We'd bought the house to live in. We used an agent to help us, and we ended up with a small loss each month. We had to top up the cash each month to cover the mortgage. Lorraine continued to work as an accountant and subsidised the mortgage cost by £150 per month. In a strange sort of way, we thought we were *saving* (in air quotes) the money.

Lorraine attended a business network meeting and came back from it with a new perspective. People at the meeting were talking about owning property that created an income that would be enough for them to give up their jobs. Curious to know how others made property work, we set out to find a mentor.

Lorraine knew a mortgage adviser in one of our pubs (we used to own a chain of five pubs) who was buying houses every week, using same-day refinance (which unfortunately you can no longer do). You'd buy the house cheap, then a bank would remortgage with you the same day for a higher price. This was how the older generations bought their property portfolios and built up 40-odd houses.

We learnt from mentors how to get high-cashflow properties. We learnt the whole 'buy, refurbish, refinance' method but eventually we were getting stuck. It never quite got there. There was always money stuck in property. We borrowed from investors, family and friends, and it wasn't long before we owed investors nearly £300k. We eventually paid everyone back, but it was a very painful process and one we learnt a lot from.

The refurbishments always cost more than we could refinance. It wasn't working, not until we learnt a different way. We found the answer and fine-tuned it. We've shared it with our students, who have also got the same results.

It's our belief that had we not gone through this huge challenge we would not have over £8 million worth of property today and more houses and flats than we can remember to count (circa 45). In fact, we now anticipate doubling quicker than ever. Once you get it, you can grow and grow easily.

WHAT IS THE SECRET?

The secret to the whole process is the idea of momentum investing. There is more detail behind this, and the method and process are discussed in later chapters. The high-level view is the idea that you start with one lump sum of 'risk capital' – it could be your savings, your inheritance, your business profits or investors' funds. You buy one property, add value and then refinance, get your funds back out and invest in the next property. You create momentum in your investing by being able to move from one property to the next without the need for additional funds.

It's the idea of recycling cash: your initial deposit and refurbishment money moves from one house to another. It creates flow and energy in your investing.

Momentum investing requires patience, as it needs you to wait for the right deal. You must buy a deal, not a ready-made investment. There is a difference. When a house developer sells a property, they do so for profit, and so they have taken the profit and equity out already for themselves. Now you need to do this for yourself.

“

Momentum investing requires patience, as it needs you to wait for the right deal.

”

We say that you can tell a good property from the picture – if you just look at the picture, you can tell that a property is 'smelly.' Imagine a well laid-out show home, with cushions and throws. The last thing you can see in this image is a smelly house – and definitely not urine or that damp and mouldy 'old house' smell. We like to buy smelly houses. The smelly house will most likely be discounted compared with other high-quality homes in the area.

As you might have realised by now, when it comes to property investing, there are a lot of different strategies you can use in order to make money.

Momentum property investing is all about taking advantage of the opportunity that exists in the market in order to purchase multiple properties in a short period of time. When you are looking for properties to invest in, it is important to look for the right properties. The property should be located in a good area with solid prospects for future growth.

It is also better that the property owner should be looking to sell quickly. They should not be looking for the best price in the market, because they will wait for that to happen. Typically, if the property is their main home, there is normally a motivation to get the best price to buy the next home. They are less likely to be motivated to sell at a discount.

Circumstances where homeowners may be less concerned about price include when they are:

- **Facing divorce**
- **Embarking upon emigration**

- **In mortgage arrears**
- **In some financial crisis**
- **Unwell or needing to sell their home to fund care.**

In other words, there is some more pressing need, where time and certainty are more important than the price. It is important to move quickly and make an offer before someone else does. In most cases, the seller will be motivated to sell quickly and will be more likely to accept your offer.

If you are able to purchase multiple properties using the momentum property-investing strategy, then you can really speed up the process of building your property portfolio.

The next stage of momentum property investing uses the idea that you have increased the value of the original investment property, and then leverage the increase in equity by taking it out with a refinance of your mortgage, to then move on to the next deal.

Most investors who don't understand this principle get stuck after one or two deals. They can find just enough deposit money and cash to buy their first property, and then they get stuck.

CAN YOU HAVE YOUR CAKE AND EAT IT?

Can you have capital growth and high income from one property? This is the ultimate 'have your cake and eat it' scenario. Have your cake and eat it implies some kind of greed, but when have you ever bought a cake and thought *I'm not going to eat this?* Property is a win–win situation – you get to financially benefit and you provide homes for those that need them.

The traditional buy-to-let property was the mainstay of the investor looking to get better returns than in the bank. However, house prices have increased, the deposits needed have increased, but the rents haven't increased in the same way. Whereas house prices on average double every 10 years, rental prices don't typically follow the same trajectory. According to a report and index from the Office of National Statistics for October 2022, UK rental prices have increased by 15.6% since January 2015.[14] Using data from the Office of National Statistics for November 2021, the UK average house price rose by 41.98%.[15] House prices are growing over three times faster than rental income. So the returns on buy-to-let properties have dropped accordingly.

There are two main calculations for property: return on investment (ROI) and yield.

ROI is calculated as:

The annual net profit divided by the initial investment × 100 = ROI%

ROI is used to tell us how hard our money is working in the property.

Yield is calculated as:

The annual rental of the property divided by the purchase price of the property × 100 = Yield%

Yield is used to tell us how hard the property works to generate rent. If yield is high, the rent is high compared with the overall value of the house. If yield is low, the rent is low compared with the overall value of the house. It tells us the performance of the house.

This is why it is challenging to make single buy-to-lets work: the yield (see later section for explanation) is being pushed down by strong growth in capital values that is not matched by similar rent increases. The formula is becoming bottom heavy.

In addition, we need to consider the rules and regulations introduced recently for buy-to-let properties and the ability to obtain mortgages. With the introduction of the Prudential Regulation Authority (PRA) in April 2017, landlords now must demonstrate that their rental income covers typically 125% of their monthly mortgage interest payments. Mortgage lenders all have slightly different variations of the test, and you should check with a broker what products and criteria you and your property need to meet.

The stress tests ensure the property can cover the mortgage payments, if rents increase and with extra interest costs, voids and arrears. So, even if you could afford the property, it may not be possible to get finance for it if the rent is not high enough.

The switched-on property investors are now looking for higher cashflow and value-added strategies. This could be through developing the property, doing a refurbishment or even converting it to multi-let accommodation, like houses in multiple occupation (HMOs; house shares – a high-cashflow strategy) or serviced accommodation (think Airbnb). There are definitely still opportunities out there for those looking to invest in property – you just need to be creative and use the right high-cashflow strategy to make it successful. Find your property strategy by completing the property strategy worksheet in the Property Millionaire Planner.

There are many reasons why traditional buy-to-let properties don't work any more:

- **Property prices have increased, meaning the deposits needed have increased and rents haven't increased in the same multiples.**
- **The rules and regulations around buy-to-let properties have changed, with landlords now having to demonstrate that their rental income covers 125% of their mortgage interest payments, meaning that refinancing has become trickier, and cash is getting stuck/left in properties.**
- **Investors are now looking for higher cashflow and added-value strategies.**
- **New taxation rules, whereby investors can no longer claim all of their mortgage interest back, have made some properties, and even whole portfolios, unprofitable.**

However, interest rates are still fairly low; investors can get better returns from property than they would if they were just putting their money into a bank account.

So smart investors are still looking at property to invest but, to have their cake and eat it, they are looking to other high-cashflow strategies rather than single lets. With high cashflow each month, you are having the cake and eating it. For example, with HMOs we would aim for at least 10–15% ROI, and most HMOs yield at least 10% on property values. If you want to replace your income, then buying lots of single lets is not going to get you there. You can't refinance to get all your cash recycled back out and your income is so low that it's difficult to scale. High-cashflow strategies can be used by new investors, and you will typically need to own your own home to get a mortgage.

The Property Millionaire Method applies to high-cashflow strategies like HMOs, serviced accommodation and blocks of flats.

HOW DO YOU ADD ROCKET FUEL TO YOUR PROPERTY-INVESTING JOURNEY?

We were recently challenged by someone who was considering investing in property that they didn't want any debt. Their primary concern was that mortgages were bad! In his groundbreaking book *Rich Dad Poor Dad,* Robert Kiyosaki writes about the idea that there is good debt and bad debt. Good debt can buy you an asset that makes money. Bad debt is a loan or mortgage that buys a depreciating item, like a car, and doesn't give you money.

If you are borrowing money to pay for your lifestyle, or you are remortgaging and using that money for holidays, then you are consuming your money. This is bad debt. You need to be creating assets that give you income and returns, not consuming assets.

Good debt is like rocket fuel that can help you launch your property portfolio further than you could do on your own.

The job of a business is to take an investment of capital from shareholders and create revenue and profit back to the shareholders. The very nature of a company is to invest and deliver profits. It's very important to make a profit. It's very important to not make a loss. Business is not easy. Running a business can be hard work. Losses can be made in business, just as much as profits can be. Therefore, running a business carries a risk.

When you buy a property for let, there are two types of return: capital growth and income. When buying with a mortgage, the rental income is used to cover the interest payments on the loan.

Some people might not have the money saved up to buy a property outright, so they take out a mortgage and can get into the property market sooner, without having to save up for a long time.

Whatever your reason for using a mortgage, it's important to understand that it can be a very beneficial way to buy property. Banks and lenders see property as security and then they are able to lend fairly cheaply. This is because mortgage interest rates are so low. You might be able to buy multiple properties with the same amount of money that you would have used to buy one single property, which means you will grow much faster.

As your own investment in the property is just the deposit, you can generate more income for every pound invested in the property. This inevitably leads to a higher ROI when using leveraged money.

Rick uses an analogy of how your initial risk capital – that pot of money you are holding right now – is like an army. You are about to send them out into battle to come back with some more money. Every £1 you have working that is invested in higher ROI deals, the more money your army brings back in.

We always use ROI and yield when investing to make decisions about how to use our money. Yield is a measure of the income-generating performance of the property, expressed as a percentage. Remember:

ROI % = Annual Net Profit / Initial Investment × 100

Yield % = Yearly Rental Income / Property Price × 100

Yield is a good metric to use when looking at which area to invest in; it helps you benchmark a good rental area against the capital values of the properties. This helps you to choose between a good rental property in Birmingham or one in Manchester. In this way, yield is extremely important to get the best possible chance of driving a good return.

But once we have settled on an area, we then use ROI to decide which property deal to invest in.

We want to make an important distinction here.

The ROI equation tells you how quickly your 'investment' comes back to you. If your ROI is 100%, that means your annual net profit is the same as the initial investment. And, because it is annual, it also tells us how many years our investment will take to come back to us: if ROI is 100%, it will take one year to get our investment back. Of course, not all deals are 100%. They are typically a lot lower, but we won't invest in any deals that are not at least 10% ROI.

If you divide the ROI percentage into 100, you will get the payback time in years.

For example, if your ROI is 20% (a typical high-cashflow property strategy, that uses a mortgage too), this means it will take five years to get your initial investment back, because 100 / 20 is five.

But if your ROI is only 5% (a typical single let, perhaps a flat purchased outright), it will take 20 years to get your initial investment back, because 100 / 5 is 20.

By just following a few rules and processes that create value in your property deals and combining with high-cashflow strategies, your property investing could realise you 20% returns. You are saving the difference between 20 years and 5 years.

You are saving 15 years.

HOW TO TURN A NEST EGG INTO A MILLION?

If you have lots and lots of cash sat in the bank, choosing the best-yield area might be the only decision you need to make. But not everyone has enough cash to buy lots and lots of property. To obtain the most properties and leverage your money, you will need to use mortgages.

We looked at the numbers about leverage, and the impact of rocket fuel (using mortgages) in your investing journey. We wanted to substantiate what we knew intuitively already. We set out to understand what the loan-to-value percentage (the effective leverage) does to the ROI. The average UK house price and rent were included. This was applied to different investing strategies and at different mortgage interest rates.

PLEASE NOTE: You need to contact a mortgage broker and understand your situation and the risk of taking on a mortgage. The following examples are purely for demonstration of the power of leverage. The PRA regulations prohibit you from achieving maximum leverage due to rental cover as the maximum mortgage you are allowed to take out is restricted to a stress-tested X% interest with 125% rental cover needed; your lender will have different criteria depending on the mortgage product. The examples demonstrate the effect of loan-to-value percentages on the ROI.

Single-let property

Although we know the average UK house price is higher and the UK yield is lower, we are going to use £250,000 to demonstrate the calculations. As we've already said, we believe you should be buying below average house price properties where you can look for multiple ways to add value. The average house price includes expensive areas and large properties that we won't really consider for investment purposes. Average UK rental numbers have been used, and although we would mostly aim to be operating in the top 5% of market rents, the average has been used; this seems a fair assumption to make. The numbers are merely a demonstration of the power of leverage.

This is the single-let property at 3% interest rates. Interest rates are going up and down. The following table helps us understand why single lets have been working for some investors despite the low yields of single-let property.

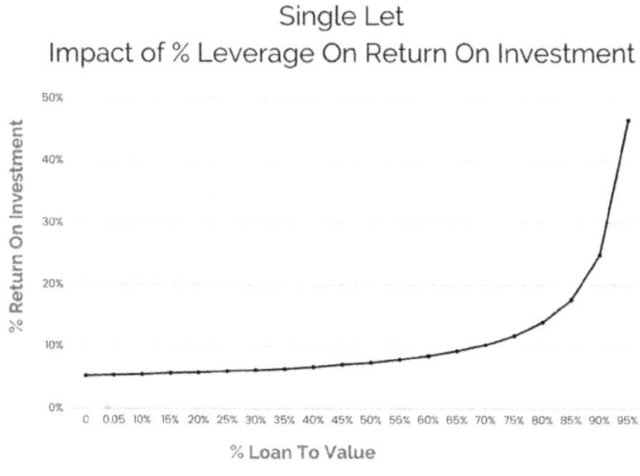

Loan To Value	Return On Investment
0 (no mortgage)	5.2%
50%	7.3%
75%	11.7%
85%	17.5%

As leverage increases, the ROI / profit percentage significantly increases. In fact, at 100% leverage the return is infinite, since the ROI calculation is therefore dividing by zero – as none of your cash is left in. Notice that the higher the loan to the value of the mortgage, the higher the ROI.

Mortgage interest rates have been very low globally, and have recently increased to over 5%. This will be the highest they have been in a long time – since 5 July 2007, in fact, when they were 5.75%.[16]

Next, this is the single-let property at 5% interest rates. Note the yield is 5.2%.

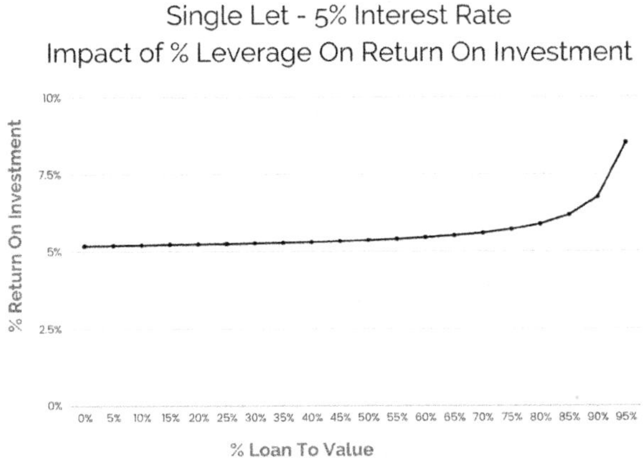

Loan To Value	Return On Investment
0 (no mortgage)	5.2%
50%	5.3%
75%	5.7%
85%	6.2%

This is the single-let property at 6% interest rates. Note the yield is 5.2%.

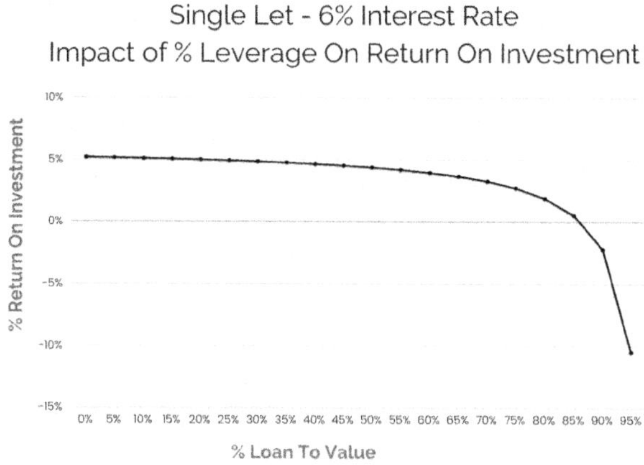

Loan To Value	Return On Investment
0 (no mortgage)	5.2%
50%	4.3%
75%	2.7%
85%	0.5%

Effectively, the ROI is now reducing with the higher LTVs. What most investors don't realise is that, as the mortgage loan to value increases, their cost of money is higher than their yield. The property itself can't generate (yield up) more than 5.2%

cash per pound of value, and therefore it starts making a loss, as 6% is higher than 5.2%. This is why most single lets don't work: because the yield is not high enough to jump over the cost of money. The returns become marginal. Your deposit is the only part of the house price earning any money!

What does this mean to you?

You should take a view on whether you think interest rates will continue to increase in the long term. If you think mortgage interest rates could go higher than the yield in your area, then you will want to consider the percentage of loan you take against the property. It would seem prudent to limit the loan to value on properties where the yield is low.

For example:

1. **50% LTV at 3% interest rate: you would make £765.50 per month gross cashflow or 7.3% ROI.**
2. **50% LTV at 5.0% interest rate: you would make £557.17 per month or 5.3% ROI.**
3. **50% LTV at 6.0% interest rate: you would make £453 per month or 4.3% ROI.**
4. **If you only had funds to buy one house and bought it without debt, you'd have £1,078 per month.**
5. **If you bought two houses and used 50% LTV, you would have £1,531.00 per month at 3.0% interest rate or £1,114.34 per month at 5.0% interest rate.**

If you buy one house with no mortgage, it generates £1,078 per month.

If you buy two with 50% LTV, you'd have £453 per month more cashflow at 3% interest.

If you buy two with 50% LTV, you'd have £36 per month more cashflow at 6% interest.

But you would also lose out on a huge capital growth opportunity; if house prices were to increase by 25, 50, 75 or 100% in the next 10 years, you'd lose your equity created in the second property, from £62,500 to as much as £250,000 (depending on how much house prices increase).

Instead of having two properties which could double in value in 10 years, you would only have one. Your debt doesn't double. You keep the equity. This is why they say the rich get richer, because the rich use debt to grow their wealth and it compounds over time. Imagine if you bought 10 houses: the range increases from £625,000 to £2,500,000!

The table below shows the potential capital outcomes, and purely for demonstration purposes, if at the start you had £250,000 you can see how using debt makes you richer over time. If you don't have these funds, then you can work with investors in joint ventures or other ways of controlling property.

1 House	House Price Now	House price in 'x' when Doubles
House Price	250,000	500,000
Mortgage	-	-
Net Equity	250,000	500,000

2 Houses	House Price Now	House price in 'x' when Doubles
House Price	500,000	1,000,000
Mortgage 50% LTV	250,000	250,000
Net Equity	250,000	750,000

4 Houses	House Price Now	House price in 'x' when Doubles
House Price	1,000,000	2,000,000
Mortgage 75% LTV	750,000	750,000
Net Equity	250,000	1,250,000

You need to watch yield in single-let properties, in relation to the loan to value, as if it is too close to mortgage interest rates, you won't beat the cost of the money over the maximum yield and income the property attracts.

Multi-let property

The calculations are based on a house price of £250,000 and an average £495 per calendar month rental, and they have been used for a five-bed HMO.[1] Due to the fact that you have more

[1] We'd always recommend the six-bed HMO, as that last room makes such a difference to the long-term profitability, but for this example we are being prudent with a five-bed HMO.

commitments to bills, in this scenario we are taking net rent into account and have made a deduction for utilities and repairs and, at this stage, no mortgage interest costs.

This is the multi-let property at 5.29% interest rates. We've used 5.29% because generally lenders have a higher interest rate for multi-lets or HMOs.

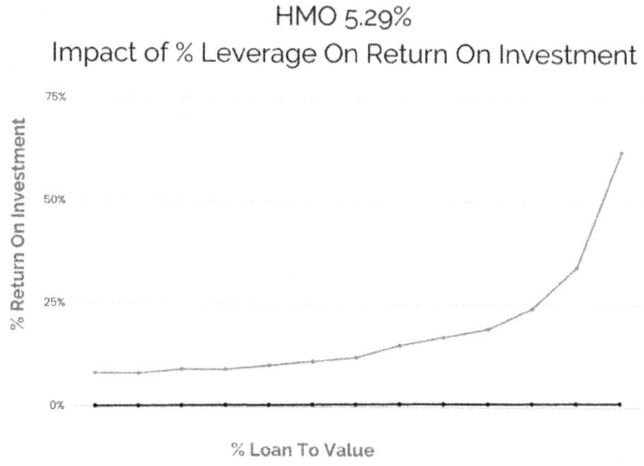

Loan To Value	Return On Investment
0 (No mortgage)	8.1%
50%	10.9%
75%	16.6%
85%	24.1%

And as we saw in the previous example, because the yield is higher than the cost of the money (the interest rate) the ROI will be higher and the more highly leveraged the investor because you are making a margin over the cost of money.

If interest rates increased to 7% this graph shows the same impact.

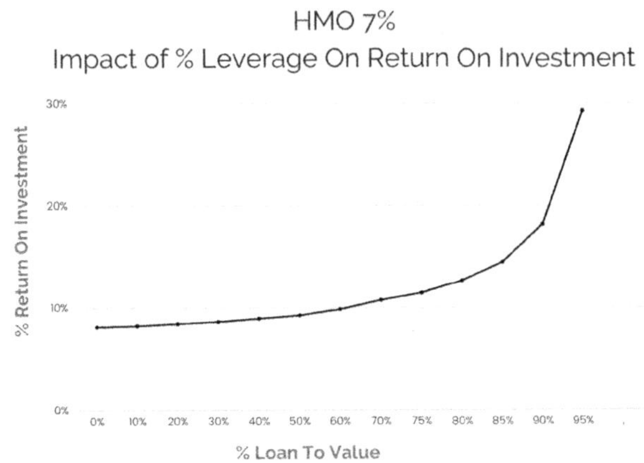

Loan To Value	Return On Investment
0 (No mortgage)	8.1%
50%	9.2%
75%	11.4%
85%	14.4%

The ROI increases the higher the loan to value because we are still beating the cost of the money (the interest rate) by the yield. In this case, the ROI increases exponentially to infinity as you go to 100% ROI.

What does this mean to you?

You should take a view on whether you think interest rates will increase in the long term. If you think mortgage interest rates could go higher than the yield in your area, which is important for the type of property you are investing in, then you will want to consider the percentage of loan you take against the property.

It would seem prudent to limit the loan to value on properties where the yield is low. The opportunity to achieve 16.6% at 75% loan to value, which is a great return, or 11.4% at higher interest rates, this loan to value would mean four houses could be purchased with the same capital sum.

For example:

- **With 75% LTV at 5.29% interest you would make £863.44 per month or 16.6% ROI.**
- **With 75% LTV at 7% interest you would make £596.25 per month or 12.6% ROI.**
- **If you only had funds to buy one house and bought it without debt, you'd have £1,690 per month.**
- **If you bought four houses and used 75% LTV, you would have £3,453.76 per month at 5.29% interest or £2,385.00 per month at 7% interest.**

However, now putting all your money into one property and not using leverage effectively costs you £1,763.76 per month and the lost opportunity of capital growth, which is now looking much more serious.

Instead of having four properties which could double in value in x years, you would only have one. Your debt doesn't double. You keep the equity.

The table below shows the potential capital outcomes.

1 House	**House Price Now**	**House price in 'x' when Doubles**
House Price	250,000	500,000
Mortgage	-	-
Net Equity	250,000	500,000

2 Houses at 50% LTV	**House Price Now**	**House price in 'x' when Doubles**
House Price	500,000	1,000,000
Mortgage 50% LTV	250,000	250,000
Net Equity	250,000	750,000

4 Houses at 75% LTV	**House Price Now**	**House price in 'x' when Doubles**
House Price	1,000,000	2,000,000
Mortgage 75% LTV	750,000	750,000
Net Equity	250,000	1,250,000

In summary, this is the power of leverage, as long as you respect that this is debt that you are taking on, and that there is the risk that if you don't keep up your mortgage repayments your house could be repossessed. In some ways, this model is both simplistic and complex; it doesn't include any costs of the risk of taking on tenants, it doesn't look at inflationary pressures or tax implications. There are some important considerations to recognise, namely to respect yield, interest rates, loan to value, but to invest based on ROI.

This section may be overly complex for some, but the lesson to take away is that leverage helps you. Leverage is the ability to take a small lump of money and literally 'lever' that as deposits of 25% to leverage 75% of the mortgage against the property. Some people don't like debt and we understand that. But this section was to show you how powerful mortgages and debt are in growing your personal wealth. This is literally why the rich get richer – because they have more funds and cash to leverage.

THE BIG EXIT PLAN

If you plan to hold property for your retirement, you will need a plan to pay off the mortgages. It is debt, and the lender expects their capital to be returned!

There are two main ways to sort out the mortgage repayment:

1. **You could switch to repayment when you have reached your 'ideal' size of portfolio. You should also be looking to do this in good time before retiring, as a repayment over 12, 20 or 25 years is very different in terms of cash going back to the mortgage company. Work with your mortgage broker on a plan for pay down. Ideally, that would be a good number of years ahead of when you plan to no longer work.**

2. **You could sell half your portfolio and pay the debt off on the other half, keeping that half. This does rely on property prices going up, which is not guaranteed, although there should be at least 25% equity in your properties, as lending is usually restricted at this level. This does mean there is a**

risk that you will have to sell all the portfolio to pay off the mortgage. You will need to sit down with a tax accountant and go through the plan and plan for your tax bill, too, which could be substantial.

Leverage is good for scaling, but you do need to have a plan for exit or for how to retain the property without debt. This way you can retain the property and the income. However, before you are overwhelmed, it just requires a little bit of planning and thought when you start, so you can put that into action and ensure everything is perfect! You gotta have a plan!

SUMMARY

We once had a lump sum of about £80,000 – it was the money from one of our pub sales. We didn't really know what to do with the money as we had been accidental landlords. At the time we still hadn't pieced together the 'property investing' puzzle, so we decided to buy a car with £40,000 – cash. It was a lovely blue Audi cabriolet. It was a lot of fun. That was the first week. And then it sat on the drive. And our lump sum of money slowly corroded away sat on the drive. Yes, we drove it and we enjoyed it. But did we enjoy £40,000 worth of car? I don't think so. Rick bought a private number plate, which was about £7,000. The stuff that we spend our money on is momentarily exhilarating, and then we have to pay for it or continue to fund it. That money could have bought two or three properties at that time, but now the car is long gone. We could have an additional 50 properties now.

Invest in assets that earn you money. Save every penny. Get a lump of cash together. Scrape and scrimp now to get into property. It will buy you freedom and time in the future. If you think it's too late to start, then you are wrong. It's never too late. On average it takes 10 years for property values to double. You may enter at the wrong point, as prices have just been through a growth phase, and it might take longer – maybe 15 or 20 years. Absolutely none of it is guaranteed. Nothing.

If your health isn't strong enough to get into property, then we completely understand. But get into property to help your life force. Have time to walk the dogs, stroll on the beach, buy a beach house or go travelling. The real truth is it's not about the money – it's about what you do with your time when you have the money.

Having your cake and eating it is all about having cashflow every month, the potential for long-term growth in capital values and being able to scale a property portfolio using leverage. Why would you bake a cake and not eat it?

CHAPTER 3

WHAT IS THE PROPERTY MILLIONAIRE METHOD™?

Property is all about detail, and in that respect, there is a lot to consider. We want you to think of this process as like baking a loaf of bread. There are some ingredients you just need to make a loaf of bread. You need flour and yeast for the bread to rise. Then you must follow a recipe to make dough. You also need to wait and prove the bread for the yeast to activate and start creating air bubbles in your dough, ready for baking. You then need to bake your bread. Every step is simple, but you have to follow the recipe and process. It might take a while to get it just right, and there may be a few flops and disappointing results, but then it clicks into place and you make it work. Perfect!

OVERVIEW OF THE PROPERTY MILLIONAIRE METHOD

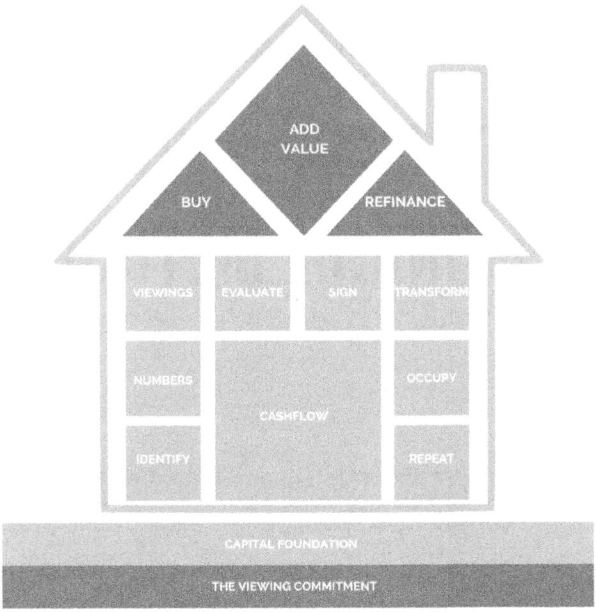

There are four parts to the method. Only two are active, with things you need to do; the other two are principles you apply in your investing.

The active part includes things you need to do on a day-to-day basis:

1. **Viewing commitment – two viewings per week, in quarterly sprints. Each sprint should result in a property owned.**

2. **The INVESTOR Process, which is a step-by-step process. This is the way we obtain, acquire and cashflow property.**

The passive part includes things you need to understand and apply. This is the unconscious know-how and knowledge that will generate huge wealth. It's the difference between investing accidentally and investing on purpose.

These two are the foundations and the roof of your house. You need these to be there or else your house will fall down – and a house with no roof is not watertight and will be ruined.

1. **The BAR Principles™**
2. **Capital and Cashflow Foundation™ – the underlying theories that make the Property Millionaire Method work**

The property market will punish you and put you in a 'no cash' prison, stopping you from achieving financial freedom, if you do not follow the BAR Principles and understand the Capital and Cashflow Foundation. This will mean you are building your property portfolio on quicksand, so nothing will be certain, and you will become overwhelmed.

The passive part is like learning the property-investing language – learning the letters and the spellings to be able to speak the language. If you do not apply these two to your property deals, you will run out of money, and you won't be able to give up your job or retire. They are the lightbulb moments that you will then realise have made other people multimillionaires.

Once you understand the BAR Principles and the Capital and Cashflow Foundation, what you actually need to do is follow the eight-step INVESTOR Process, combining that with the viewing commitment, and then we will be cooking on gas!

In later chapters, we'll discuss the different parts in detail, but we'd like to give you an overview of all four parts now.

CAN YOU EASILY BECOME A PROPERTY MILLIONAIRE?

Viewings, viewings, viewings. It's that simple and that difficult. Your property millionaire journey starts with viewings. Nobody should buy a property without doing a viewing. The person who views the property doesn't have to be you – though ideally it would be – but your interests in the property need to be served by a physical 'in-person' viewing from someone. Viewings help you to build your confidence, understanding the existence of massive opportunity in the property or recognising the lack of potential it holds.

Some owners market their property and are market ready. They are sat on the property portals like Rightmove and Zoopla waiting for prospective buyers. Some property owners actively search for buyers. We are looking for leads from existing landlords, owners and sellers, and we are trying to attract them to work with us, convincing them that we should buy or perhaps even lease their property.

It is just common sense that not every property you see is going to work for you or that the owner won't always be prepared to drop their price to one that works for you. We need to consider this a business and, in any business, a lot more people don't become customers than actually become customers.

According to Marketing Sherpa, 79% of marketing leads never convert into sales.[17] Some deals never work.

You can actively market leads, and Rick's book, *45 Ways to Buy Property*, covers 45 marketing ideas to find property deals and leads, either on or off the market. The number of agreed sales as a percentage of offers made is always going to be less than 100%. We understand that at the beginning of this journey there is a lot of excitement and enthusiasm, and then the rejections hit; 10, 20 or 30 noes later, and your motivation has depleted. You were hoping for a bit of beginner's luck but all the rejection has killed your motivation.

Sometimes we do get beginner's luck and sometimes we are tested in our resolve. That's why we have monitored our students' results and we know what the secret sauce is for those that do well.

Students who got two to ten deals per year done actually went on an average of seven viewings per month (1.65 per week).

Students who achieved one or less deals per year done actually went on an average of 2.5 viewings per month (0.48 per week).

Literally one extra viewing per week makes all the difference in results. This demonstrates the importance of effective business habits.

Given that an average viewing takes 20–30 minutes, this represents an additional 1.5 hours' work per month (or 18 hours per year) in order to **achieve twice the results.**

That is on the basis that we aim to only do deals that are worth a minimum of £500 pcm in net cashflow/profit.

An additional 18 hours spent on viewings translates into an additional £6,000 profit per year. How many 'lots' of 18 hours of viewings would it take to get you to your financial goals? You have to be really careful how you spend your time. Work on high-value activities.

We also know that slow and steady wins the race.

Doing 50 viewings in one week is not realistic. You are less likely to follow up every viewing with an offer and negotiate to your best ability. Cramming viewings doesn't work, just like revising for exams the night before; we know that we needed to do the work and should have started months ago. What does work is finding two great properties per week and going to view them. Book the viewings in your lunchtime on Mondays, do them on Saturdays. A business that has a rhythm, something that happens week after week without effort, is more successful. It's all about creating effective business habits.

Some of you will see some variations because it does depend on your local market, current market conditions and how well you are positioned for cash, mortgages and other finance.

As modern-day entrepreneurs, we are impatient. We seek instant satisfaction once we have made a decision. It's easy to see why 35–50% of sales go to the vendor who responds first.[18]

If you are looking for an idea of the level of success you can expect, then let's look at 100 enquiries for property deals. This applies to properties on and off the market.

Out of 100 leads (on Rightmove, Zoopla, leaflet responses, direct-to-vendor letter enquiries):

- **38 are sales ready (i.e., they will consider your offer, if you like the property)**
- **14 will become qualified prospects (i.e., you negotiate and try to make the deal work for both parties)**
- **4 will convert to sales/deals.**

This means that only four out of every 100 enquiries or leads convert into deals. It takes many noes to get to a yes – in fact, it could be 96 noes before four of them convert. Lots of noes eventually lead to a 'yes', so celebrate the noes.

To become a property millionaire, you need four property deals at £250,000 (remember the average in the UK is higher) to own and control £1,000,000. From the figures above, to get these four deals you will need to do 100 viewings. If you do two viewings per week, then you will have done 104 viewings in a year. The Property Millionaire Method™ is therefore amplified by your activity.

TWO VIEWINGS PER WEEK = 4 PROPERTY DEALS = £1 MILLION PROPERTY

If you achieve four properties, you are considered a portfolio investor in the UK by the PRA rules. If you could do four deals per year for 10 years, you could reach 40 properties. In fact, we think once you've started you will find that your property numbers increase quickly.

Two viewings per week is more than achievable; it's the Goldilocks zone of just enough to get results without killing you in commitment and effort to get results.

Focus on '52 weeks is 104 viewings, and we only want four deals, that's 100 noes.' When you get a 'no' from an offer you put in or a lease option proposal, then just smile at it. Recognise that this is just the next 'no' and it is just another one ticked off before you get to that 'yes.' Tenacity wins.

One of our mantras is 'just one more thing.' It's 'how can I do one more thing today that gets me a little closer to my goal?' Many a deal done is the result of this one idea.

Your one more thing is:

'TWO VIEWINGS PER WEEK'

“

Two viewings per week is more than achievable; it's the Goldilocks zone of just enough to get results without killing you in commitment and effort to get results.

”

CAN YOU FOLLOW EIGHT SIMPLE STEPS - THE INVESTOR PROCESS?

This is an eight-step process that you follow and take action on to get the properties into your portfolio. We'll look at it in detail in Chapter 6, but the eight steps are:

- **Identify**
- **Numbers**
- **Viewings**
- **Evaluate**
- **Sign**
- **Transform**
- **Occupy**
- **Repeat**

Identify

How to 'identify' your first steps into property. Where do you invest? What areas? What property strategy are you sourcing property deals for? Identify your reason why. Motivation can be transient. We look at how you can attach to a reason why to help keep you going in spite of the rejection.

We also look at investing areas and strategies to identify where to start, and how to buy the right property for investing and not because you would live there.

Numbers

We take a deep dive into the numbers and simplify it for you: how to invest and what metrics to use. In property you need cash and capital to invest to start with and move into positive cashflow. Making a small loss each month means you will have to supplement your property investing from other sources, meaning that you therefore cannot scale. How hard is your money working for you?

Viewings

The number of viewings is important, but so is knowing how to do a good viewing. What to look for? You need to be methodical, looking out for potential costs and opportunities. What's the potential? It's not about the décor, so you need to get away from that idea. The smellier the property, the better, as there is normally more opportunity to add value.

Evaluate

How do you move from a viewing to making an offer? What due diligence do you need to do? How much should you offer? Can you be creative and make an offer that doesn't require lots of deposits? Perhaps a lease option or rent-to-rent offer?

Sign

You've got an offer accepted, so now you need to pull together the contracts and legal paperwork to move forward. How can you work with other people's money legally? Always document anything that involves other people's money, including loans from friends and family. What paperwork do you need?

Transform

Once you've got the property, it's important that you aim to maximise your returns through design. Create desirable properties. Find the perfect builder. Demystify health and safety legislation, building regulations, fire regulations and licensing. Simplify the process.

Occupy

Finding the 'ideal' tenants means less work, low arrears and less hassle. To make the money, you have to be able to deal with tenants and guests. You've got to be able to collect the rent and systemise the routine. Find easy ways to get the best tenants without any hassle.

Repeat

Business is about rhythm and creating a pattern that repeats itself every month. Simple systems and processes can generate cash straight into your bank account.

Property investing should be a systemised repeatable process. How do you refinance? How do you ensure there is no money left in deals? How do you build up a portfolio? What is your cookie cutter? Momentum investing – tick – job done!

CAN YOU RAISE YOUR GAME? THE BAR PRINCIPLES

The BAR refers to the game-changing principle of 'raising the BAR'. It is how investors raise their game and raise the standard (and the bar) on their investing activities. They increase the value of their properties. It's what makes the difference between investing slowly and investing with momentum.

Since we've been training property investors for the last decade, we've taught hundreds of people to build their own momentum portfolios using the BAR Principles. We created them to help people understand how they can grow and scale a property portfolio with limited funds. Even investors with large sums of money for deposits eventually run out of money, and these fundamental principles work wherever you are investing.

How can you level up to being a property millionaire by following the BAR Principles?

The important outcome is generated by you levelling up at each stage and moving the bar a little bit higher as you get more deals under your belt. Using this process, you can make sure that you are investing in the best properties and getting the best returns you can. Investing in property requires skill, and the BAR Principles help you deliver fantastic returns on your investment.

There are three steps to BAR. If you miss any of them, momentum property investing does not work. The three steps are:

- **Buying well**
- **Adding value**
- **Repeating and refinancing**

The overarching principle is to create equity by forcing it into the property valuation.

Anyone can spend money on property.

You can buy lots of really cool fittings and spend lots of money. However, nobody said the property needs to be vanilla or boring, so you need to spend your capital wisely. You need to create a brand and a design that stands out.

The reality is that property investing is not about being cheap and charging the highest price to the point that it is unethical.

It's about balancing the costs with the value delivered, aiming for a high-value product.

A lot of investors don't invest with a ROI mindset. They invest for a monthly cash amount. This is a short-sighted view, as this will not measure how well you are using your money.

As we repeatedly say, property is about detail; you need to get the planning permission and the building regulations correct, along with the niche, the brand and your product. What do we mean by a 'product' in property? Any property that you buy and intend to turn into cashflow is a product. It's a package of services, goods and value that someone will buy.

People who don't understand these principles don't invest in property for very long. They buy one house, do it up and renovate it, then they have to sell it to realise the profit. Any profit is often not enough to replace a salary, and the cash is often needed for the next project. Put simply, they added some value to the property but not enough. Their product didn't have the wow factor.

ORGANISING YOUR ARMY - THE CAPITAL AND CASHFLOW FOUNDATION

The intention of your property investing is important. You need to consider where you are starting from and what foundations you are building on. Do you have capital? Do you have equity? Do you have any cashflow? Some people have zero in both capital and cashflow and that's why it's important to understand your starting position and where you want to go.

Stephen Covey, in his book *7 Habits of Highly Effective People*, wrote, 'Seek first to understand.' This is an important first step. Understand you. What is your situation? How can you start in property? Where are you going? What is the strategy?

We truly believe you can start anywhere in property, but you have to understand your position. If you have no money, then it's not really possible to buy property. You may have to learn and use strategies that involve *controlling* property without ownership. For example, your property business could lease or rent a property for your business to cashflow. Then over time you can start to buy property and have all the benefits of ownership, including capital growth. Don't be naïve around property investing; if you need money, you have to start working hard to learn about property and be investable. You must work on you and your network first. Understanding this will save you a lot of heartache and wasted time.

If you have cash and capital, how well is it working for you? Do you need your capital to grow and be reinvested or to earn you an income?

How effectively is your capital that's tied up in other property and investments working for you? Is it time to evaluate how well your capital is performing?

Every pound of money you have is like a soldier out there working for you. It should be a good solider too. The English Civil War in 1642–1651 had two English armies fighting each other over whether there should be a Royalist leader, King Charles II, or whether there should be a Lord Commander, Oliver Cromwell, leading a government and parliament. Oliver Cromwell's army, the Parliamentarians, were organised, disciplined, well trained and strategic, and they won the Civil War. The Royalists supporting Charles II had parties the night before battles, were disorganised, were lavish and unprepared. They lost. Your soldiers, your money, should be hard-working.

Great wealth isn't accidental... it is BUILT!

... one property at a time!

Organised, planned and intentional.

You have to win your financial freedom.

You have to engage grit, determination and discipline.

Be deliberate.

Create your wealth on purpose.

Do you know how well your cash, capital and equity are performing?

Are you ignoring it because you are confused? It's time to get clear.

Just because your capital is employed in a property or other asset doesn't mean that you don't need to think about how well it is working.

Why invest for capital growth? Because you have other businesses or assets that deliver your income. If your income is not reliant on you, then just investing for capital growth could suit your circumstances. It is dangerous to invest for capital growth for low cashflow. You don't want your investments to be a drag on your business, turning them into loss-making properties if interest rates or costs increase.

Your unique situation and where to start depends on your cashflow and capital situation. This is the foundation of your investing. You should never deviate from this plan, once you recognise where you are and where you are going. To do so would be like picking up shiny pennies. Keep going and adding the properties. Four properties per year is a strong target, so set the goal and shoot for the stars – you may well hit the moon.

SUMMARY

These are the four steps of the Property Millionaire Method:

1. **The viewing commitment – two viewings per week**
2. **The eight-step INVESTOR process**
3. **The BAR Principles**
4. **The Cashflow and Capital Foundation**

The viewing commitment and the eight-step INVESTOR process are what you need to do. The BAR Principles and the Cashflow and Capital Foundation are what you need to apply and understand. If you are at all overwhelmed as to where to start, then start with the Cashflow and Capital Foundation.

CHAPTER 4

THE CASHFLOW AND CAPITAL FOUNDATION™

Maybe you are overwhelmed by property. You might even have one or two buy-to-lets that don't make any money.

Perhaps you have a lump sum, a pot of cash, or savings that are sitting in the bank not doing very much except being eroded by inflation.

You are confused by high capital values in your area, and what to do next.

In fact, overwhelm is pretty common in property investing, as there are just so many choices and decisions.

This chapter is about your cashflow and capital foundations, and how to step back and find your wealthy future.

Whether you need the income and cashflow of property or not, you should always invest in property that you intend to hold, that cashflows first and is profitable, and then is used for capital growth second. Cashflow is a safety net against market changes. Property that is cashflowing can weather market conditions or interest rate increases. It can be largely irrelevant what the market is doing if you have bought for cashflow.

WHAT IS CASHFLOW IN PROPERTY?

Cashflow is the stacking of all your costs against your income and still being left with surplus. Most properties at some point in time will experience a void or arrears from tenants, or unexpected big repair bills. Cashflow is a cushion against that. Negative-cashflow businesses are like an aeroplane being two degrees off course and flying the wrong way around the world to get to its destination. It's just going in the wrong direction.

Having a property that cashflows as a negative means that you need another income source to top this up. If you lose £200 per month in your properties, then that's £200 you have to earn somewhere else to cover the losses.

Our first property that we let to tenants was actually a home we bought for ourselves. When Rick got a promotion, we had to move to a new area and we couldn't sell the house, so we ended up renting it out. At first, we topped up our mortgage payment and covered the shortfall between the rent and the monthly mortgage payment, seeing this as savings. But five or more of these properties, and that would be a significant chunk of money to find each month. You must only buy property that cashflows – the more it cashflows each month, the stronger the position you will be in; more investors will want to buy your property, and if it is 10 or 20% ROI, that means you will have earnt the same amount in income in 10 years or five years as money that is invested in the property. High-cashflow income property that provides 10–20% returns is very achievable if you follow all we are teaching you here. Contrast that to 2.5 or 5% ROI from single-let property and you will find that you will need to wait up to 40 years for your earnings from that property to return 100% of your invested capital. And that's without considering inflation and cost-of-living impacts.

Nobody we know can ever sit down and work out what their future looks like from a retirement point of view, as they don't know what life will look like in 20 years' time. But how can you make decisions today without understanding, in detail, how much income you need? Do you have enough savings? Where will you live? Will you downsize or upsize? Will you move to a cheaper capital area?

HOW MUCH CASHFLOW DO YOU NEED?

Do you need extra income to top up a pension?

Do you want to create a legacy for your children?

How old you are and where you want to be when you retire will determine the urgency, speed and pace of your investing. A 25-year-old can afford to make the odd mistake and recover, whereas a 55-year-old needs to get the next 10–15 years spot on.

We have designed a spreadsheet tool that will help you look at all these decisions. The importance of this is that it will help you make decisions today that will guide you in a straight line to retirement.

Decisions today are easier if you know, for example, that you are going to sell your business in the next 10 years. Whoever buys your business won't have you around to do all the things you do, so you have to plan a way for the business to become self-sufficient, making yourself redundant in the process. If the sale proceeds from your business aren't enough to give you income, then where does that money come from? Now you can see a gap, you know how big that gap is and can start working on solutions to fix it.

Often people who do not understand property look at successful investors and ask the question 'How have they done that, without a huge lump sum of money?'

To some extent, knowledge and patience are the two most important ingredients. You will never scale a property portfolio without cashflow.

But scaling profitability is the only way to grow a portfolio, so they *must* cashflow. Two loss-making properties that become 30 loss-making properties is just a door to bankruptcy. And, we think, a huge waste of your time.

Why build a portfolio that doesn't make money?

Most people we know who want to invest in property have a desire to get their freedom and time back. They recognise it's not about the money; it's about the time and freedom that money buys you. People are motivated by money as far as what it buys them. The stuff and things that you can buy with money are often a temporary mood repair, making you feel great for a day or two; then it's just stuff. The Cashflow and Capital Foundation is about where to start and focusing on what suits your situation and your circumstances.

You can keep doing the same old thing, and nothing will change. You won't notice much difference. You will still go to work and keep driving the same road to get there every day, live in the same house with no prospects of change, have the same car and holidays every year.

We believe most people seek growth – personal, financial and emotional. How can you control your destiny, income, future, wealth or time?

There is always a **cost of doing nothing**! If we use an average house of £250k, and the average increase in price has been 10% per annum, there's a clear example. If you failed to own or control four houses (either purchases or lease options) you would be looking at a *loss* of £100k wealth, and if they were HMOs, this would be a lost income of between £24k and £48k.

It's not about refurbishing property and spending lots of money to make it a show home and selling for a quick £20k profit, because for someone with a lump of money sat in the bank, while you have grown it slightly, you've just made the problem worse: you now have a bigger lump of money! It's still not working for you. You should be working it – there is a difference.

We want you to learn how to use your savings or borrowed investor funds over and over.

COMPOUND INTEREST, INFLATION AND INTEREST RATES

When most people think of making money, they think about working hard for it. While this is certainly true, there is another way to make money that is often overlooked: compound interest. Compound interest is one of the most powerful tools in an investor's or saver's arsenal, and if used correctly, it can help them to achieve their financial goals.

Compound interest is simply interest that is earned on any previous interest that has been earned, as well as on the original investment.

There are two main ways to take advantage of compound interest: through saving and investing.

Both saving and investing are important aspects of building wealth, and it is important to understand the difference between the two. By taking advantage of compound interest in property, you can grow the equity in your property. For instance, let's say your property is worth £100k at a compound interest rate of 5%. The 5% interest is the average house price increase for the property in your area. After one year, you would have £105k (£100k property + £5k in equity/interest). In year two, you would have £110.25k (£105k principal + £5.25k in equity/interest), and so on.

However, the important thing is that debt does not compound and grow, as long as you pay off the interest as you go. Your property value will compound and grow, but your debt will stay the same. Plus, if rental prices go up, your income will increase to cover your debt interest and, effectively, inflation erodes the value of the debt.

It's a complex economic concept that has a significant impact on our daily lives.

Inflation is a sustained increase in the general level of prices for goods and services.

How does inflation erode the value of money? Inflation causes the prices of goods and services to increase, which in turn reduces the purchasing power of money. For example, if the average price of a loaf of bread increases from £0.50 to £0.60 over a period of time, then the number of loaves of bread you can buy with £1 decreases.

Why is debt not inflationary? Debt is often confused with inflation, but they are two different concepts. While inflation is a sustained increase in the general level of prices, debt is simply an amount of money that is owed by one party to another. So, while inflation can erode the value of money, it will not increase the debt amount. Over time, because it actually erodes the value of money, it in turn erodes the value of the debt relative to the time period.

One example of how inflation can erode the value of money is when it causes prices to increase faster than wages. This can cause people to struggle financially as they find it harder and harder to afford the goods and services they need.

Another example is when businesses raise their prices in response to increased costs. For example, if the cost of materials or labour increases, then businesses will often pass these costs on to consumers in the form of higher prices.

- **If you are on a fixed income, such as a pension or salary, your purchasing power will be eroded by inflation.**
- **If house prices go up by 10%, you will need 10% more deposit.**
- **If you are saving for retirement, inflation will reduce the value of your savings over time.**

However, when we invest in property, property prices tend to increase over time to match wage growth, material costs, market sentiment and other factors that make property investing such a powerful concept.

MONEY WORRIES - TOO LITTLE OR TOO MUCH

The Goldilocks zone

You may be surprised to know that when people have too much money, they often worry about how to protect it and make good investments so that they can continue to grow their wealth. They are well aware of how much inflation is decreasing the value of their money. Inflation at 10% per annum and interest rates at 1% effectively means you are losing 9% of your savings each year.

Having a lot of money can be scary, and people start to worry about losing it. You may have concerns about how to stop inflation eroding it. Some become so frugal they worry about spending any money and become worried about making any investment. For those who have never had money, they would think this situation is impossible. Trust us when we say this: we have a friend who was left a large inheritance and he eventually spent it all on just living, some years before he retired. There was a window of opportunity to invest and use some for living expenses, but he held on too tightly to the money, worried others would take it all away. The person who took it all away was him.

On the other hand, when people have too little money, they tend to worry about things like how they're going to afford food and housing. This is because when you don't have much money, every penny counts, and you never know when you're going to run out. But people in this situation sometimes make bad choices, such as spending money on things they don't need instead of saving it for later.

So, in a way, you could say that having too much or too little money makes people worry. And while this may not be a fun thing to think about, it's still an important topic to consider. After all, money is a big part of our lives, and how we handle it can have a big impact on our happiness. Property investing can help; if you have money parked in property and earning you a cashflow, you can relax that your cash is working hard for you.

“

Inflation at 10% per annum and interest rates at 1% effectively means you are losing 9% of your savings each year.

”

In general, we think that having either too much or too little money is not ideal, and it can create pressure when you're in one of these situations.

THE EMOTION OF MONEY

Often money is hard earnt from savings, working hard, going without, scrimping and being stingy about what you spend your money on.

Someone who has spent years foregoing the luxuries of life and avoiding frivolous spending will not want their sacrifices to be in vain and will be keen to see their funds working hard too. Deciding what to invest in can be a real challenge.

Lumps of money can come from probate, inheritance and divorces. In all these scenarios there is a lot of emotional baggage that is weighing down on the beneficiary. Families fall out over wills and inherited property. Siblings squabble over the decisions and whether property should be sold to pay for their parents' care bills.

There is a lot to think about; perhaps you are struggling to decide whether to invest in property, hold on to funds in the bank or whether to release equity in your property. In reality, unless you invest and grow your money for yourself, a lot of your net worth will be inherited by your children, partner or family and paid in inheritance tax or towards your care bills in old age. What are you waiting for? What do you really want from your life? Property is life-changing for the relative passivity of it; with it, you can create time freedom and financial freedom. Please note we are not saying it is 100% passive – there is a lot to do – but you get to decide how and when you work, although getting that property portfolio means there is a lot of work up front.

Some people sit on their capital and take no risk. That in itself is a risk, because you are now allowing inflation to erode the value of your money and, while everything else is increasing in price, you are experiencing the paralysis, like a rabbit in the headlights. Instead of running away from the car, you are staring into the lights, too scared to keep going.

The idea that having debt is risky often paralyses some people. The rich get wealthier because they use debt (the bank's cash) to leverage their smaller pot of cash.

Think of your deposit as being like having either a shopping basket or a shopping trolley when you go to a supermarket and the supermarket says you can fill your trolley for free. Your risk capital can help you lift much more weight than you could carry in your arms. Whatever you start with really helps. The larger your starting pot of cash, the more you can leverage and invest.

YOU HAVE TOO MUCH MONEY, SO WHAT DO YOU DO?

The answer is simple – invest it! If you have a lot of money, it's important to find a way to leverage it so that it can work for you, so you don't have to. Just like energy, if you keep your money in one place it will go stale and be wasted. You need to put it to use so that it can make more money for you!

There are a number of different ways to invest your money, and it's important to choose the right option for you. You may want to consider putting your money into gold, stocks, bonds, or mutual funds instead of property. No matter what route you decide to take, it's important to do your research and make sure you're comfortable with the investment strategy you chose. You really need to know your stuff.

We joke that the only two things we are good at making money with are business and property (Rick will also say Rolex watches, having doubled the value of his Rolex collection in the last five years). The point is to learn and invest in what you know. Don't dabble in crypto because your mate has made £80,000 on it. You could easily lose £80,000 and not know how or why. Volatility is much more evident in crypto – so prices go up and down. It's not unheard of for crypto to crash overnight because of some tweet that Elon Musk has made. The number one rule is to invest for value. An asset that delivers value and has value is hard to beat.

If you're not sure where to start, talk to a financial adviser. They can help you to figure out what type of investment is right for you and give you some advice on how to grow your money. It's important to remember that investing isn't always easy, but it's worth it in the long run!

There are many different investment strategies out there, so make sure to find one that fits your goals and risk tolerance. With a little bit of effort, you can make your money work for you and achieve financial success!

YOU HAVE EQUITY, SO WHAT TO DO?

You may have equity in your home or other properties, but what do you do with it? There are two main ways to get money out of your property: selling it or releasing equity. Each has its own advantages and disadvantages, so it's important to understand them all before making a decision.

If you're looking to retire and need income, then you could consider downsizing to release some cash. You'll be able to get a lump sum of cash that can be used for anything you want. However, you will have to find somewhere else to live. If you're not ready to move, then releasing equity may be a better option, although you will owe more money in debt and have to pay interest each month. You will then need to find an investment that will beat the rate of interest on your equity release and that will give you a regular income, or your funds will be invested in another property, if you choose to buy a house. However, you will need to pay down your house, if this is your main home before you retire. Plus, while you'll still own your property, your home will be at risk if you don't pay back the money you owe.

So, which option is right for you? It really depends on your personal circumstances. However, releasing equity is a great way to get money out of your property without having to sell it. It means you could invest in other rental properties that generate you more income and cashflow.

If you're thinking of releasing equity, there are a few things you need to bear in mind. Firstly, the amount of money you release will depend on the value of your home and how much you still owe on it. You'll also have to pay back the loan over time, so make sure you can afford the monthly repayments.

Releasing equity isn't right for everyone. Make sure you understand all the options before making a decision. And if you're still not sure, talk to a financial adviser and mortgage broker who can help you to figure out what's best for you.

YOU HAVE NO MONEY, SO WHAT TO DO?

So, you want to invest in property but don't have any money? It's a common problem, but there are ways to get around it. You can borrow money from a finance company or attract investors who will give you a loan or partner with you on a joint venture. Whatever route you choose, you do need to make sure you borrow money from investors legally! There are rules about joint venturing with investors from the Financial Conduct Authority (FCA) called PS13/3 (see page 158). So be careful and do your research before choosing this path to property ownership.

Focus on finding the best deals! With a little effort, you can find properties that will make you a healthy return on your investment. So don't give up on your dreams of becoming a property investor just because you don't have any money! There are ways to make it happen. Most investors have no money to invest in property at certain times, because they have funds in deals, or they are waiting for refurbishments and refinances to go through.

One option is to borrow money as a loan. This can be a good way to get started in property investing, but make sure you read the terms and conditions carefully, so that you know what you're getting into. It's important to be able to afford the monthly repayments, or you could end up in a lot of debt.

Does money go to money? Money and your personal profile (how people see you in the public domain) are linked. What often happens is people will watch from afar, they will not comment and then, once they have built up enough trust about what you are doing, they will reach out to you. The more people you tell about what you are doing, the more money you will attract for your deals.

THE FOUR INVESTOR TYPES

To get started in property, you need to understand your own personal circumstances and what to do first. The following investor archetypes will help you to learn this.

Profiling to get returns – the profile investor

If you have literally no funds to get started in property, then we want to help you. We started with less than £15k cash, and most of that we invested in our education. When you are starting with no funds, then you must build up your profile and make this your biggest asset. If you ever run out of funds, you must return to being a profile investor. The profile investor must first invest in getting their profile out into the world.

People will invest in others who they know, like and trust. To do this you must create and maintain a personal profile. You can do it through social media and networking. You never know who is watching you and who has funds to invest. Family, friends and colleagues are often keen to invest, once they see what you are doing. But you have to show them. Finding ways to start without deals or properties can be tricky. But investors can get quite lonely on their property journey, and you'd be surprised at who will come out of the shadows and offer you money to get some of your deals done. You need to learn how to find deals and pitch to investors, so that you can get the financial freedom and wealth you desire. This is entirely doable.

Profile-first investors need to literally focus on their personal profile online or in networking circles. You have to be able to attract investment, and for that to happen you have to tell everyone what you do. Don't be scared; many, many people have attracted funds to themselves with less effort than you might be thinking. Having a strong personal brand is essential if you want to attract investors to your business. Your personal brand is the first impression potential investors will get of you, so it's important to make sure it's polished and represents you in the best possible light.

If you can create a positive image for yourself, investors will be more likely to invest in your business. A strong personal brand shows that you're credible and invested in your own success.

Creating a good personal brand takes time and effort, but it's worth it in the end. Make sure you stay consistent with your branding and always keep your target audience in mind. If you can do that, you'll be well on your way to attracting investors and growing your business. Whenever you are in property investing, creating a profile is a rewarding process, and can be a huge asset for you in the future. Some people we know have waited to look for investors until the point when they have the deal ready to invest in – this is too late. You will always find the money for great deals if you have spent some time investing in your profile. However, if nobody knows who you are, or they can't like or trust you, then you will never find the money, no matter how great the return.

Tips for creating a strong personal brand:

1. **Define your personal brand. Know what's important to you (e.g., great communication; honesty; commitment and doing what you say you will do).**

2. **Stay consistent with your branding. Make sure the look and feel of your business is consistent across all platforms, from your website to your social media profiles. You want people to recognise you for a colour, background, etc.**

3. **Make sure your branding presents the essence of what you are known for. What makes you unique? What do you want potential investors to know about you? Once you have a clear idea of what your personal brand is all about, you can start promoting it effectively.**

4. **Connect with your target audience. Know what your target market is and create content that appeals to it. This could be anything from blog posts to videos to infographics.**

5. **Be active on social media. A strong social media presence is key for building a strong personal brand. Make sure you're active on the platforms your target market is using, and post regularly.**

6. **Stay up to date with trends. Keep an eye on the latest trends in your industry and make sure your branding reflects them. Post about news and events happening in property.**

7. **Get involved. Volunteer help, answer questions, share other people's posts (make sure you credit them), comment on great posts, and make sure you mention people on your social media profiles. This will help you to build a strong network of connections and show potential investors that you're involved and trusted by the property community.**

8. **Be yourself. The most important thing about branding is to be true to yourself. Don't try to be someone you're not, because it will come across in your branding and people will see right through it. Be authentic and genuine, and your personal brand will shine through.**

If you want to attract investors to your business, a little effort will go a long way. Access some resources on how to build your property pitch and your networking pitch in the Property Millionaire Planner.

The need to build income to scale – the income investor

Income investors typically start with a modest pot and need to find creative ways to get going. You may be able to *control* property without buying it. This will require you to learn about lease options and rent-to-rent investing strategies. Sometimes we've seen others buy buildings that do not replace their income, so they are looking to flip but only because they think they need to grow their risk capital first. While this can help, it's also taking the long route. They are really stuck in 'shiny penny syndrome', picking up any opportunity in property. This is where the income seeker needs to be really disciplined and patiently seek out the *best* properties to *replace* income. You don't want 'lumpy' money strategies, giving you a lump sum in a year's time; this is *not* the objective. You must pursue the high-cashflow strategies, because it is *only* once you have replaced your income that you can do some of that other fun stuff – flipping, developments and refurbishments. Cashflow is king and it buys your freedom. If you already own a few properties and have not hit the income goals you need, then it might be time to sell or refinance some of those properties, to kickstart your investing income strategy properly. Otherwise, don't buy one house and then get stuck; it's better to wait and buy the right property and get educated in high-cashflow strategies, so that you can then have the 30-plus property portfolio in 10 years' time.

Momentum investing – the creative investor

This means you will risk your capital pot. You have a modest pot of cash to get started with but, much like the income seeker, you can probably buy one or two houses using mortgages and then your cash will be gone. You can see ways that you can make money, but for your long-term success, the ability to keep recycling your cash is key, as well as not making any mistakes, or buying the wrong house and getting stuck. You must follow the strategy of BAR: buy well, add value and refinance. One single let will not replace your income or help; you *must* momentum invest by refinancing and getting all your cash back out. If not, how will you buy the second, third and fourth houses? You need momentum investing to grow the 30-plus property portfolio. You need to invest with skill, knowledge and pace. Get into a flow and you will soon grow that pot of cash into multimillions. The key for you is to build your deal-finding skills and get your deal stacking turned around quickly so you can put lots and lots of offers in to get those deals over the line.

Investing a pot of cash – the capital investor

This requires a large pot to get going, and to scale quickly. You have a great pot of cash, but counterintuitively this might actually be stopping you from *investing*. That cash has come to you with a lot of emotion, whether through a legacy or by being hard-earned, as there is often a huge amount of your emotion invested alongside the actual money. So you don't want to waste it or make the wrong decision.

Often a mentor can make a real difference to your success; just having someone who supports a decision to buy a house and says 'yep, I'd buy that property' can often be the difference between procrastinating and adding rocket fuel to your property-investing journey. With some careful decision-making, you must follow the strategy of BAR: buy well, add value and refinance. One single let will not replace your income or help you refinance to get all your cash back out to buy the second, third and fourth houses. You need high-cashflow strategies. You need momentum investing to grow the 30-plus portfolio. You need to invest with skill, knowledge and pace. Get into a flow and you will soon grow that pot of cash into multimillions. The key for you is to build your deal-finding skills and start stacking your deals quickly. Then you can share your ideas with a mentor, so once the first few deals get done, you create confidence and skill to *really* kickstart a hugely successful property portfolio journey.

ROCKET FUEL FOR YOUR PROPERTY-INVESTING JOURNEY

There are many ways to control property – of course, everyone thinks of a traditional property purchase. However, there are a few other ways you can control property for your benefit, even controlling the property without ownership.

The secrets of buying property with none of your own money

The first thing to say, of course, is that money will be needed to get into property. But this is about buying property with none of your money and using other people's money or other organisations' money to fund purchases and refurbs.

The six ways of doing this that we're going to cover are:

- **Using banks**
- **Rent to rent**
- **Asset finance**
- **Lease options**

- **Investor funds**
- **Creating joint ventures.**

Banks

Banks tend to like traditional property projects, in terms of lending, so they will want to see conventional development models. We see the BAR model working well here:

- **Buy – houses in need of refurb or that are in poor condition**
- **Add value – fix problems, make new and borrow funds to develop**
- **Refinance – this is taking the increase back out of the property with a mortgage product, so your initial risk capital can start again on another property.**

You may need to combine this source of finance with another source for it to be a genuinely cash-free deal. Banks tend to be more conservative and typically may fund up to 75–80% of a project. You will need to source the balance elsewhere, and check with your mortgage broker about how to use loaned funds, as the bank doesn't want you to be 100% leveraged or borrow all the money to invest.

Rent to rent

This method uses the owner's tied-up capital. It's where you take a property and give a guaranteed rent to the current landlord or property owner, and then rent out at a higher amount and make a profit on top.

Typically, this could be a single-let property that you turn into a multi-let (HMO). This means the combined rental on individual rooms being rented should be higher than the payment of guaranteed rent to the owner.

Technically, you don't have ownership of the physical property, but you get to control the cashflow for a secured period.

It is also an opportunity to buy from the owner in future – a strategy we have employed many times.

Asset finance

If your property business already has assets, or if you are a limited company, you may be able to apply for asset finance. The clue is in the name, though; you will need to have some form of asset to offset the finance company's risk.

You might also be able to use the property you are refurbishing as collateral for borrowing the funds to do the actual work. This will depend mainly on the equity in the property and how much an asset finance company will lend.

Other forms of asset finance could include you leasing furniture, if you needed it for an HMO project, or furnished serviced accommodation.

There are several asset finance and development finance companies, so do take some time to look around and make enquiries.

Lease options

Lease options involve you getting a property and buying/paying for it an agreed number of years later. The owner is effectively using their property equity and supplying the house to you. It offers you the option – not the obligation – to buy the property at a fixed, agreed price.

With lease options you will need to pay for a solicitor and there will be a small nominal consideration but, essentially, this is a low-cash property strategy.

Investor funds

Through networking and meeting more property people, you will find a number of investors. These investors could be cash rich and time poor, but they are looking for better ways to generate a return on their money. They will lend you money, if you build up enough confidence and present the right opportunity to them. However, you can't just find an investor overnight; it takes time to build a trusting relationship before you go into business with someone. Complete the investor and financing worksheets in the Property Millionaire Planner to help you keep track of interested investors.

Going to investors directly can be quite daunting. One of the critical pieces of advice is to know your numbers and make sure you can answer questions. If you don't know the answer, say you don't but that you will find out. Building good investor relationships can be a great way to expand your business. Once you have completed a few successful projects and made everyone money, they are likely to want to reinvest with you.

Joint ventures

Fifty–fifty joint ventures with parties are about coming together to provide equal value. You don't necessarily have to bring the money. If someone has the money but no deal, no time or no know-how, then they don't have anything without you. This is the mindset you need to have with a joint venture. It needs to be a partnership where both parties understand the value the other brings.

Most effective joint ventures are between two parties that are missing something. Three things are needed for a joint venture to be effective:

- **Time**
- **Skills (sometimes finding the deal itself is the skill)**
- **Money.**

It could also be something as simple (for you) as providing the build team, the planning know-how, the knowledge or the potential to manage the project.

If you have the time and skills to buy good deals, then a joint venture partner can help you with the cash. As a so-called armchair investor, they might be busy running a business or some other venture that requires their focus.

Always get a contract to understand what is happening on the project and make sure everyone's roles and responsibilities are clearly defined. It is better to have this and not need it rather than need it and not have it.

As you can see, there are several different ways to raise finance; they can be combined or used to help you invest and generate revenue from property without having a large pot of money to start with.

Property investors have a wide range of options available to them, so do look at those that fit with your situation and make sure that your decision matches your strategy.

Research here is vital; don't simply rush in because you feel you need to get the deal done.

CASE STUDY - VICTORIA MILLER (PROFILE INVESTOR)

'Honestly, one of the main challenges I've overcome is that I was doing property in secret for many years. I think it was partly because of a lack of confidence that I didn't want to tell everyone I was investing in property, not until I felt credible; I worried about how I would look on the outside, especially as my first job in social work was in housing, and I worked with the homelessness team. I didn't want to be judged – I was afraid that people would think I was being greedy by investing in property alongside having a full-time job.

'At the end of 2019, before the pandemic hit, I had been in a place of analysis paralysis for about 12 months. I thought I'd learnt all I needed to learn about strategy, but I wanted a mentor and signed up for Rick Gannon's 12-month membership programme. He encouraged us to tell everyone what we were doing. If it hadn't been for that push, I probably wouldn't have done it. It has been such a journey because, until that point, I didn't have a website or a Facebook page for the business and nobody knew what we were doing.

'When I eventually told everybody, it was completely fine. I had built this whole story in my head that wasn't true; I was welcomed to the community and so many of the people around me have been incredibly positive and supportive. People seem to want to know more and are interested in working with us as joint venture partners or private investors. I'm glad I did it. I'm so grateful for Rick, who helps me to see there isn't any kind of problem in regard to what other people think of us. The support from everyone and the sense of community was a big help. I did an investor pack and raised funds.'

HOW TO GET STARTED

If you are in analysis paralysis, not sure where you are, then please review the Property Millionaire Planner and check out the flowchart to see which investor type you are.

SUMMARY

By working out what you want and what resources you have, there is an easy path you can follow, and you can understand what you need to do next. People very often tell us they are confused and overwhelmed by property, and they don't know where to start.

You can do anything you want in property, but the smart way to work is to get your income needs covered first and forever, not just for the next 12 months. Then, once you have achieved this, you can work towards another level of income which might give you a lot more towards your personal ambitions or goals. It's not about the money but what the money can make happen for you.

PART TWO

MONEY

Income, savings, money and cash; all of these have a huge impact on your life. Property is unique as an asset class, where particularly in the UK, we have an insured government-backed system that means a person who owns land can be certain that this is the case. This means huge amounts of money can be leveraged off the back of property assets. Money is everywhere and, once you understand how to create the flow and energy needed to help others with their money problems, money will never be an issue for you. You may not believe us, but if you quit chasing the money, and focus on helping those who have money to get better returns, invest their money and put it to good use, you will never be short of money yourself.

Let's discuss in the next section how to use money.

CHAPTER 5

THE BAR PRINCIPLES™

BUY WELL

What do you need to do to get a great deal on a property?

A common saying in the property industry is 'You make your money when you buy, not when you sell.' Basically, this means that the price you pay for a property is the major factor determining your profit later on. We all know the importance of keeping costs down. Imagine that a projected cost for a refurbishment was £50k but you managed to be really careful with the costs and save 20%. In real terms you would have saved £10k, but if you are buying a house and buy 20% below market value on a £200k house, this is a £40k saving, which is massive.

Some of you may well be thinking that in certain markets it's not possible to buy anything below market value.

Well, we would disagree.

We did two viewings this week (the market is very hot right now): one was to a property that was listed four days ago, another was to a property listed five months ago. The agent of the second property actually said that they were extremely motivated to sell. Not only had the second property dropped its asking price from the first time it came on the market, but the vendor was now considering dropping the price again and taking offers on the revised price. The drop was £175k on a £900k starting price, a drop of 19.4%, due to motivation. In contrast, the first property that we saw had block bookings of 10 different buyers in one day, and was actually half the size of the other one we'd seen but not half the price. As expected, the new listing that had people clambering over it went for over the asking price, and we are negotiating on the other to get a good deal. Time changes motivation, and you should always look for properties where the owners are indeed becoming more motivated.

There is no point in relying on the state of the market or wishful thinking. It all comes down to finding great opportunities.

We buy well when we look for four things in a property deal.

The best properties to buy are ones that:

1. **Have a good rental demand, so you can be sure of your monthly income**

2. **Are located where prices will rise (good capital growth), so you can release equity later**

3. **Are being sold by a motivated seller, so you can get a discount**

4. **Are in a high-yield, niche area of the town or city, where rent is high but house prices are relatively low. There is always an area that is above average yield for your city, because that is the nature of averages. Spot it before you start.**

Not all four things are needed in every purchase, but they make it much easier to become a property millionaire.

There is no point in buying property 50% below market value on a Scottish island with no electricity or supplies in the middle of the North Sea just because they are a motivated seller (an extreme example, but we hope you see what I mean). A bargain isn't always a bargain.

Good rental demand

Demand is the key to getting a good rental income. You want to be the best operator at the top of the market, with the best product, and you want to be generating above-market rents because everyone wants to rent your property.

You will have fewer voids (empty rooms, flats or houses). Voids are often overlooked as a cost to the business, but it is vital to avoid them to ensure the long-term success of the property.

Getting a room or property rental income that's above market value increases your profits. The higher the rent, the more profit. Typically, a house still has the same maintenance and running costs, so the extra rent goes straight to the bottom line.

Now, it's time to talk about a word that's knocking around in the private rental sector at the moment: saturation. You might have heard people are starting to say that the market's oversaturated, which means that the rental demand is less than it was before because the supply has increased. Actually, that's not true. That is just an individual perception. The market is busy, but it's never been any different. Now go back and do your research: 15 years ago, people were talking about market saturation.

There's always room in a busy market. People will always need homes and with a housing shortage in the UK, underlying demand is good. You just need to be confident in your area.

If you go to the mid-range of rents, that's where most of your competition will lie. If you go above that into the high range of rents, then you've got less competition because you are not competing on price. You are now offering a higher product, so it's likely you can populate your rooms more quickly and keep them occupied for a lot longer.

Areas with good capital growth

You want to focus on investing in the right areas. You need to think about where your tenants will want to live, not where you would want to live. This is not your dream home, or your ideal location or your ideal commute or catchment area – it is where tenants want to live.

Good capital growth happens where the market is developing as an area that more and more people want to buy and live in. There is normally an influx of investment in the area. This could be an area about to get a new Amazon warehouse, where lots of new jobs are created, or an area that is benefitting from a government-funded scheme, such as a new train station or new infrastructure allowing people to get to jobs and places of work easily.

My property students who don't do their due diligence often become procrastinators in the future. If you are not confident in your area, then, later on, you will become nervous, delay decisions and potentially pull out of deals.

Seller motivation

Motivated sellers are people who are looking to sell quickly and, if needed, below market value. They have a real need to sell their properties. Motivated sellers are often looking for speed and certainty in a deal because there is some other emotional or financial need to get rid of the property.

Use the Property Millionaire Planner to help you plan out your marketing and help you to plan your yearly, monthly and weekly campaigns.

Some typical lifestyle motivations:

- **Divorce – When a couple are going through a divorce, they may want to sell the marital home as soon as possible so that they can both move on and start again.**
- **Illness, death/probate – Similarly, someone who has inherited a probate property may want to make a quick sale as the house may hold sad memories.**

- **Job relocation – The employer is normally picking up the tab on moving expenses and offering a relocation package. Empty houses are a worry for people, and they have a new job to get on with.**
- **Upscaling/downscaling – A home or house that is too small or too big is emotionally charged with the feeling of not being able to cope with the property, and owners often feel in a nightmare scenario.**

Some typical financial motivations:

- **The owner has debt/mortgage arrears and needs money quickly.**
- **The property needs renovating/extending/improving and yet the owner has no money to do this.**
- **Large structural work has been identified as being needed, which is costly (e.g., roof repairs, subsidence, cracks, new timbers, repointing the chimney).**
- **The owner's chain has broken, but they still want to proceed – so you can step in and buy the property. Many, many studies are done on deals that have been agreed and then fallen over. Typically, 25–35% of agreed sales fall over before completion, which is a lot. One in three of the deals you don't win or get outbid on is going to come back on the market.**
- **The owner has run out of funds.**
- **The owner has a tax bill to pay.**

If the property was previously rented out, there could be a few specific scenarios where a quick sale is needed:

- **The existing landlord has no capital to refurbish, so they are now in the position of only being able to get low-quality tenants and low rents. Or they may have problem tenants or long voids.**
- **The existing landlord wishes to retire/sell their portfolio.**
- **The existing landlord has had a bad experience with a tenant and may have lots of emotional tension around their investments.**

High-yield areas

Invest in an area with a good yield and/or in a part of the city or region that has a great yield compared with the rest of the city or region. Yield is rent divided by property purchase price, so this equation demonstrates value for money when it is a high percentage.

Wherever you live, there will always be an area that has high value and another area of poor and low values. Low-value areas may well be less desirable due to geographical features or high crime rates or poor-quality housing. The trouble with investing in the cheapest areas is that there is lower rental demand, and this then means you can't get area-busting higher rents if you do a stunning refurb. The house is always in that cheapest area, and it pulls the top achievable rent down. We tend to find there is always an area just above the cheapest area that offers good-quality housing and where demand is not affected. This is the sweet spot. It creates huge value for you in your portfolio, and you are able to scale and grow more successfully because you have identified this area. Your rents and cashflow can be area-busting, bringing you the best profits, and your tenants will stay longer.

Start to make a spreadsheet and look at local parishes/wards within your city area. Your local council website should be able to identify the names and areas. Then look for properties and rental values. Then there is some donkey work to do: you need to visit each area and score the area for its feeling and vibe. Do you feel safe? Are there places to visit? Are there nice restaurants and cafes nearby? Are the amenities nearby of good quality? Are there parks and green space?

Use our sweet spot investing sheet to help you record and find your investing area.

ADD VALUE

What is adding value?

According to Toyota, a single car has about 30,000 parts, counting every part down to the smallest screws. The difference between the total cost of those parts and the sale price of the car is due to the skills, knowledge and ability required to put together the car. You can do the same by creating a home of sound structure that's in good repair, with a good legal title and fantastic design and layout.

Simplistically, the industry refers to the process as refurbishment. The strategy commonly known as 'buy, refurbish, refinance' (or BRR) is often a simple way of explaining the process. We prefer to refer to it as BAR because it helps you understand that not everything you do creates value over and above the potential uplift in value. You must raise the 'bar' when adding value. Your house valuation must increase.

So what do we mean by adding value, and how do you do it?

Fundamentally, adding value is what every business does. Adding value to a product or providing added value in a product can be defined as creating the difference between the sales price and the cost of the goods or service being sold. When goods or services have unique features, are of good design and are made to appeal to customers, then the price that can be charged is usually more. Therefore, adding value increases the amount of profit that a business can make.

Here's a story to explain this. Before joining my training programme, a student had bought a house up north, where the capital values are low. They purchased it for around £70,000. The student then proceeded to add en suites and stripped the house back to bricks for a five-bedroom all-en-suite HMO. The trouble with this strategy was that it resulted in a spend of another £70,000. The dilemma now was that the improvements had cost £70,000, which when added to the original purchase cost of £70,000, came to £140,000. But the value of the houses on the street was still £70,000. In order to evidence this added value, you'd have to find a way for this house to sell at £140,000 – twice the price of the comparable properties. Why would anyone buy a house for twice the price at £140,000, simply because the owner had spent money on it? There is some uplift in the fact that an investor might value that there is now a turnkey solution to a five-bed en suite, but it still will not be worth an extra £70,000.

The problem with this example is that we can all spend a lot of money on properties and houses that don't realise any extra end value in the selling price. In short, there was no added value. You are looking for the gap between costs and end value. So, is it worth the hassle or time to refurbish the property to make it worth more?

The three main ones are:

1. **Refurbishing**
2. **Knowing your market and how to add value through property strategies**
3. **Using planning permissions and planning gain for extensions so that the property can be used in the right way for your target market.**

Refurbishing

If you were to put solid-gold taps in the bathrooms of a three-bed semi-detached house in a northern town, it wouldn't make the house worth any more. Even if they cost you £20,000 extra – I'm guessing here, having never bought solid-gold taps – it wouldn't mean the house was worth £20,000 more.

If you put gold taps in a New York penthouse apartment, then that type of lavish expense and luxury could be justified in the overall sales value. So, what your market expects and the type of property it is are both important.

According to Tower Gate Insurance and their analysis of costs, the best ways to add value to homes are:

1. **Do a garage conversion**
2. **Add energy-saving measures**
3. **Convert the loft**
4. **Carry out external repairs**
5. **Remove non-load-bearing walls to create open-space living**
6. **Update the central heating system**
7. **Tidy up the garden**
8. **Paint and decorate**
9. **Renovate the fireplace and install modern solutions**
10. **Add a bathroom**
11. **Update the kitchen**
12. **Add a conservatory**
13. **Add a single-storey extension**
14. **Update the flooring**
15. **Replace/improve the roof.**

If you are on a limited budget, use it to add the most value at the lowest cost.

There may also be many other things that do not add value, instead detracting from it. These are the common property problems often found from surveys:

1. **Asbestos**
2. **Structural movement**
3. **Damp/mould**
4. **Japanese knotweed and other invasive plants**
5. **Electrical issues**
6. **Faulty drainpipes**
7. **Roof issues**
8. **Woodworm or insect infestation**
9. **Poor insulation**
10. **Flat roofing.**

What's in a design?

Lots of studies have been done about design and its effect on profitability. Businesses, on average, find a £4 return for every £1 they invest in design, according to the Design Council.

Design-led businesses outperformed the FTSE 100 by more than 200% over a ten-year period from 1995 to 2004. If design is good for big business, then it must also be good for small businesses. When we talk about design, it's easy to fall into the trap of thinking about what colours and design motifs are in fashion and how they could be incorporated into the decoration. Contrary to high-fashion design, when we design colour schemes and the interiors of properties, we are looking to find high design and low cost and maintenance. Neutral colours often last and are key for a background palette in a property. Neutral colour schemes can then always be accented with bright high-fashion colours and bold designs to create a high-end finish. The beauty of neutral background colours is that they can be refreshed and maintained easily, and then new accessories or other colours are added on top to create the interior design feel. But don't think that this is an excuse to paint a whole house in white or magnolia. If you use a neutral colour and then add bold accents to the scheme, you will end up with a house that is worth more.

We recently tried to sell our own home, and the buyer said during the viewing that she hadn't liked the wallpaper in another home she was considering buying, and therefore didn't buy it. This is hundreds of thousands of pounds' worth of purchase, and the main concern was the choice of wallpaper. Please seek out help and assistance to get a good design scheme in place. Typically, you will learn so much from this process that you might only need to hire in this skill once.

Large refurbishments

A word of caution here. Do not buy a huge property that requires a significant amount of work as your first project. You need experience to run a successful project and it can easily overwhelm the most experienced investors, let alone a newbie.

Sometimes buying several smaller houses and doing small improvements and reconfiguring the property is a speedier way to grow a portfolio than to buy one big deal. Big deals can take longer to execute and can have complex exits and could be difficult for you to control. They could even kill your property career before it's got a chance to grow. The point here is to find one or two simple ways of adding value to your property. The more complex the property, the more complex the exit. You will then be able to refinance out of the deal and start looking for your next deal.

Knowing your market

When you are adding value, you need to know your niche and market. Earlier, we discussed gold taps and the best place to put them. This demonstrates how easy it is to spend money but, in some circumstances, adding value could be about knowing your market.

A property strategy is the niche: the market you operate in. Do you create homes for students or homes for families? They both want different things, so one strategy is about house shares and hanging out together as friends and the other is about privacy and space to raise a family. You could have a holiday home strategy and be helping guests to enjoy their holidays, or you could help those with special needs and lean towards a care provider offering. The strategies are different and, if you operate in lots of sectors and use different strategies, you will often focus on too many things, which leads to chaos and confusion. As the saying goes, 'if you chase after two rabbits, you catch none.'

Learn everything you can about one property strategy and how to use the house to give 'value' to your customers. We can add value by knowing what our customers want.

If you lean into a strategy and learn all there is to know, you get good at it, you avoid mistakes and really *know* your market. This makes spotting good deals quicker, easier and more intuitive as you go along.

Firstly, get cashflow sorted. Pick a strategy that enables you to get good cashflow for both the business and you.

What income and rental strategies are there for you to create value and cashflow from a property?

There are various ways to buy and own properties, and we call these the Tools because you don't have to purchase all properties to control them and cashflow them. For example, you can control property by leasing it from an owner and then using one of the strategies below to generate the income from the property.

These are the income strategies.

Single lets

The traditional buy-to-let, where the property is let on a single Assured Shorthold Tenancy contract to a family, couple or single person. The strategy is good for new investors, but it is perhaps less profitable because of the high capital values in property, so you may need a larger mortgage to buy the property in the first place and keep some of your capital to invest in other property. However, single lets can trap you into holding lots of equity in a property without the ability to refinance to get your money back out. In some circumstances, single lets can strangle your property-investing career before it has even started. Single lets don't always scale very well. You can earn £100–500 per property per month, depending on your mortgage. It is possible to earn more, but you must take into account that this might require leaving a large amount of capital in the property.

Blocks of flats

A block of flats all on one freehold title is a great way to multi-buy residential properties. Blocks of flats on one title, where you as the owner control the building and freehold, are a good way to scale quickly. There is a sweet spot of having six flats on one title due to some of the finance products in the market. Often an investor is selling them, offering them for less than the market value of the individual properties added together.

Serviced accommodation

This is a good strategy if you live near a big city, area of natural beauty, tourist attraction, sports arena or exhibition centre, where people regularly stay away from their main home. You provide short-term accommodation that is ready for your guests to stay in. It's like a bed and breakfast but it's not, as it's for short-term guests staying away from home (i.e., it's not their main home). Technically, you can't have multiple guests (who don't know each other) staying in one property. This would then make it a bed and breakfast and so would require the correct planning permissions. The guests are one group of people who all know each other and are only short-term stays. Your income is normally higher from this type of property: you can charge £50–150 per night depending on the size and location. This could suit one-bed apartments and studios if you can find them. This is also harder work that requires good systems and coordination for guest arrivals, changeovers, bookings, cleaning, linen, etc.

Holiday lets

The strategy for holiday lets is the same as for serviced accommodation, but geared towards holiday destinations and tourist places. It lends itself to larger numbers of people staying away together. Location is key to finding a great property. It should ideally be close to tourist attractions. The property also needs to be of a high standard to attract good weekly rentals. However, sometimes you can experience the seasonality of great summer rentals but low winter bookings. Look for ways to sell winter holidays too, as this can be the difference between moderately profitable and highly profitable. We let our holiday property out fairly successfully during the spring and autumn weeks because we have a hot tub which draws guests in for low-season holidays.

Commercial tenants

You can also take your property and grant a commercial lease, subject to lender consent. Leases can be granted to businesses that want space to operate from. The type of business that occupies your property will need to have the correct planning permission; different businesses have different planning classes. Shops, takeaways, pubs, bed and breakfasts, hotels, estate agents, offices, gyms etc. all have their own use classes, and this needs to be correct to rent your property out. The government website is very useful: https://www.planningportal.co.uk/info/200130/common_projects/9/change_of_use. If you are considering commercial property as a strategy, then it is worth remembering there have been big economic shifts in how we buy goods and services because retail has been impacted so much by online sales.

We owned a pub until very recently, and the tenant rented the building from us, using the property as a pub to generate their business income. Commercial property returns are very variable, depending on the use, size, local area and planning class of the property. Some lenders also need a higher percentage deposit for commercial property. It is possible to add value by changing the use, improving the property and getting a good tenant who can pay the rent. It used to be the case that a good tenant was a high-street name that would always pay the rent and be reliable for years and decades of good rental yields, but even big names are going out of business now, so watch this space as the market adapts and changes in years to come. Local small businesses now have the upper hand, being flexible and nimble enough to change and move with the times.

You could choose to turn the property into a residential one with the correct planning permission. However, this is not a starter strategy.

There are many ways to generate income from property, and 'who' occupies the property and 'how' they occupy it affects the hassle factor and the potential returns. It's also worth noting that the usage will often determine the product that the lenders give you, and that the property's valuation will change depending on the use.

We would recommend that most investors start with residential houses. We'd go for the highest cashflow to the lowest ongoing effort strategy, HMOs, because getting cashflow sorted first is the best strategy for creating an ongoing reliable portfolio. HMOs are our favourite strategy for doing this. Avoid higher-risk large projects at the beginning. Most people with a bit of education can get into HMOs and run them successfully as a first-time investor. You will need to work with a broker on how to finance your first property and to get an HMO mortgage, but there are definitely ways of doing this.

Multi-lets/HMOs

This is where multiple individuals or a group of people share the house. Each person typically has their own bedroom and shares some of the other facilities, such as bathrooms, kitchens and living areas. This means you have a higher cashflow, as well as more costs, as you are typically covering the costs of all the bills, as the rent for the tenants is inclusive of bills. There are many different demographics of tenants who would live in these types of properties, including students at university or working professionals settling away from home for the first time and wanting to live close to their jobs.

There are many ways to generate income from property, and 'who' occupies the property and 'how' they occupy it affects the hassle factor and the potential returns.

HMOs are regulated by the council's planning and licensing departments, so you need to know what you are doing. Educate yourself before you begin so that you are aware of all the licensing and planning requirements for HMOs as mistakes can be costly and ignorance is no defence.

The returns are normally much stronger, with good cashflow. A lot of my students use this strategy to replace their income and momentum invest to grow a full portfolio. You can earn anything from £500 to £2,000 per month; perhaps more, depending on size. But they also get a lot of their cash back out of the deal, enabling them to scale quickly.

In terms of what sort of residential house you should be looking for, it is very important to contact the council, speak to the housing team/HMO officer and get up to speed on their local policies and find out whether the property you are looking at will be suitable, even if it is already an HMO. Policies change all the time, so it doesn't mean the HMO will be granted a further licence.

Things you need to know:

- **Does the area have Article 4 direction (see below)? (This will only count for new HMOs.) If it was already an HMO before the introduction of Article 4 then it would have been granted 'grandfather rights.'**
- **Does the area have additional or selective licensing?**
- **Be aware of minimum room sizes - check with your local council.**

- **Do you have enough bathrooms and toilets for all the tenants?**
- **You will need to be fire compliant, in accordance with Local Authorities Coordinators of Regulatory Services (LACORS) guidance, so you will need a smoke detection device fitted, fire doors and strips, door closers and suitable locks. Your local council can advise you on this. Even if your property does not need a licence, you will be required to adhere to this, so don't cut any corners; your tenants' safety comes first.**

After conducting your due diligence, as per the above points, we recommend that you look for houses that have a minimum of five bedrooms, or could be converted to five beds or more. People do things in different ways, but we do this because a five-bed property cashflows reasonably well and, if there is one void in this property, then we can still make a profit. If it is any less than five beds, then one void could take away all the profit.

Using planning permissions, planning gain and extensions/alterations

Planning permissions come in a variety of forms. They may be for:

- **Extension/alteration**
- **Change of use**
- **New development**

This is a very complex area of legislation. Central government writes legislation and then local councils control the process. The aim here is to give you an overview so that you can read a bit more on the planning portal and seek out professionals and a planning consultant to help you navigate the area.

You can use a variety of tools within the planning process to help you. These tools are broadly:

- **Planning applications and pre-applications**
- **A certificate of lawful existing use**
- **Permitted development**
- **Prior approval**

The way a property is used has a planning class, which could be residential, commercial, industrial, retail, and so on. If you are granted a planning class after applying for a change of use, you can use the property in a new way. This could add value because you have been through a planning permission, but it takes time and understanding to put a planning application in.

Permitted development rights are a national grant of planning permission, which allow certain building works and changes of use to be carried out without having to make a planning application. Permitted development rights are subject to conditions and limitations to control impacts and to protect local amenities. Check the planning portal and search for permitted development guidance and up-to-date information. You also need to check your local council website's planning department for any indication that the permitted development rights have been removed.

Example: permitted development, HMOs and Article 4

In some areas, councils use a piece of legislation called Article 4. This can be used by a council to remove nationally approved permitted development legislation where the council believes there is an overuse of the allowed changes, such as when it could become detrimental to the area. The council will use Article 4 to stop any further permitted development – for example, from C3 Residential use planning class to C4 Small House in Multiple Occupation, as they have decided to regulate the number of new HMOs and removed permitted development. This also means that planning use for all existing HMOs will now be more difficult to obtain than it would have been by using permitted development without Article 4.

Planning can be complex, and it is always good to get a planning consultant on board to help you to navigate the legislation and process. It's important to have an understanding of this area, as it helps you to find creative solutions to adding value to a property. If you have the time to spend a few hours reading the planning portal guidance, alongside other reading, it will help you to add value to your properties and give you a competitive edge.

Never go into a deal and invest without first getting your planning sorted. Planning permissions can take a long time to obtain. If you need time to resolve it, then consider using a lock-out agreement. This means you have secured the deal while you go ahead and get planning permission. A good solicitor should be able to help you draft and obtain a lock-out agreement while you pursue your planning options.

REFINANCE AND REPEAT

What is repeat?

Most property investors need four properties to cover their income needs. We aim for a cashflow of at least £500 per property, but this can be up to £2,000 per property if they are high-cashflow HMOs. With four properties, using this rule of thumb, your income could be £2,000–8,000 per month. The typical family income needs are in this range.

We want to grow the portfolio by repeating the process over and over, but we still want to generate an income without having to find more and more cash to invest in the new properties. The aim is to repeat this by using the value and equity we create in the existing properties in the portfolio. By repeating in this way, we will grow our net worth but we should not over-invest in the properties beyond the value created.

We are aiming to get to four properties. To grow a small portfolio requires more deposits and risk capital so you can keep investing in new additional properties. Unless you follow this process, you will need:

Cash needed for four properties = 4 × 25% typical deposit × average house price £292,598[19] = £292,598

Not very many people have funds approaching £300k.

You can add to that refurb costs and acquisition costs, such as legals and stamp duty.

If you don't repeat, it means that:

- **You will run out of deposits eventually, no matter what the size of your nest egg is.**
- **If you have investors, you will have no way to repay them.**
- **You will be stopped from buying future deals.**
- **You will use up all of your money.**

To keep a flow of deposits coming back to you, you need to look at how you can create value and then recycle it back out. In this way, you will protect your precious initial pot of money and your risk capital.

So how do you repeat?

In two words – momentum investing. This just means you can scale your business by recycling your capital through different projects. You want the majority of your capital to come back out on refinance. The more cash that is recycled, the more property you can buy. This cycle keeps your property purchasing, refurbishment and refinancing going. But, importantly, you build up property wealth, which will help you to become a property millionaire.

By investing in the best properties, your business will be liquid, with cash flowing through it, and it will give you more opportunities and income.

If you have liquid or easily accessible funds available, you'll be able to drive some attractive deals and hard bargains, as you'll be in the same position as a cash buyer. So, you can move quickly and there isn't a chain underneath you – meaning you will get chosen in preference to those with financed deals.

The three main ways to repeat are:

1. **Refinance – the bank's money. This is in the form of mortgages and other commercial lending. Banks are happy to take a charge over a property and give you money against the property value.**

2. **Rent to rent / options – other people's tied-up capital. In cases where a vendor owns their own property, you can use the property and take control of it by entering into a lease. This means you can control the use, the tenants, the rent and, ultimately, the cashflow. This is called rent to rent. You can also agree an option to purchase the freehold in the future at a predetermined price.**

3. **Investor loans and joint ventures – other people's money. You can use cash from investors to invest in property. You could go into business and form a joint venture with someone who has cash.**

We have already covered these techniques in the money section and how they apply to your financial starting situation, but specifically here we are looking at how these tools help us to scale a portfolio.

Refinance - the bank's money

Firstly, let's look at the long game – property that has historically always gone up in value.

One of the simplest ways to invest and make money from property is to buy property, rent it out and then wait. Now we know this is a very simplistic view, but if you take a longer-term overview of property, you will see that property prices always increase, and you can refinance later. This will slow your progress and sometimes life gets in the way and other things happen. It may mean you never pick it up again. But this strategy works if you have no other alternatives.

Refinancing is not something you want to do regularly as it can be costly with administration fees and early redemption charges, but if you can refinance and get another property with the money you get back out of the property, then you should consider how it will help you grow overall in the long term.

Rent to rent / options - other people's tied-up capital

Rent to rent is when we use the owner's property and step into the landlord's shoes. We take a lease or management agreement to control the property and run it ourselves.

This means we are effectively using the capital of the owner. This is a powerful strategy to use if you have now run out of money. You can invest small amounts of money to redecorate or add new furniture to attract great new tenants and rents. Importantly, you are not investing money to obtain the freehold, and you control the property with the lease or management agreement. While the vendor has no obligation to sell the property to you, we have gone on to buy rent-to-rent properties from the owners. You are naturally the first person they look to sell the property to, if they are looking to release capital or completely sell up. There are always opportunities with rent to rent, but you should not enter into a rent-to-rent deal that doesn't make a profit. The aim is to support you or your business from the cash these properties generate for you.

Additionally, you could add an option agreement to purchase the house at some future point. You are not obligated to buy, but you have the option. Your owner, and potential future seller, has to sell if you choose to use the option. This is a great way for you to use the owner's capital, give them a return but also build in some time to buy the portfolio. You can use this to agree that a proportion of the monthly fees goes towards paying a deposit. This is particularly useful if your owner wants an above-market monthly fee that is much higher than a single-let value.

Rent to rent and options are powerful tools to grow a portfolio. However, you do always need to use a legal professional to create the documents.

Investors / joint ventures - other people's money

We are not qualified to give you any financial or legal advice. However, we do want you to be aware of how you can find the right advice for the right situation, so please read the Financial Conduct Authority's (FCA) website and, if in any doubt, ask a qualified person.

The FCA introduced some legislation to protect people who might invest in an unregulated investment scheme and to prevent the general public from being mis-sold investment opportunities that might lose them their money. You need to be aware of this or you will risk breaking the law. The law is PS13/3 (https://www.fca.org.uk/publication/policy/ps13-03.pdf). The checks must be carried out every 12 months, and the evidence must be kept for the FCA.

However, a straightforward loan is outside of PS13/3. Using investors' money can be a great way to start your investing journey, but we would just caution that you'll need to consider how you will pay back your investors.

What the investor is looking for is really important. If they want a fixed-rate return but want their money back in three years' time and this fits with your timescales, then you can go ahead and get the loan agreement drawn up. Then, once everyone is happy, you can invest the funds into property. Speak to a broker first if you are considering using borrowed funds for a deposit. Effectively, you will be buying property that is 100% leveraged, and the mortgage companies don't allow you to use borrowed deposits. If you can secure the loan against a property, then this is an equity release and mortgage companies can allow this; your mortgage broker will know more.

If you are looking to do a joint venture and effectively share the profits of your investing with someone, this is regulated by the FCA, so you need to follow their guidance. There are templates in the document that will make sure you are compliant. If you are in any doubt, contact an independent financial adviser, who can certify your joint venture investor for you.

You should not talk to any potential joint venture investors until they are certified.

If you are using other people's money, then please make sure that you momentum invest and use the BAR method. Otherwise, you will consume money and not have any capital left to repay your investors. The funds could be equity in the property but that will be of little use when your investor wants paying back and, after all your hard work, you will have to sell the property to get the equity back.

How to force equity into a property and refinance by increasing the value

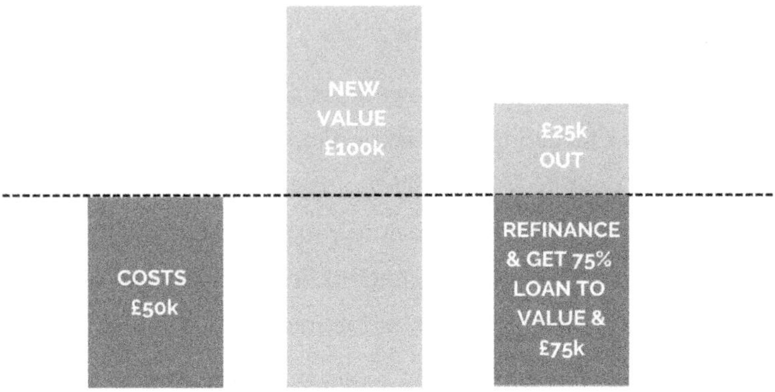

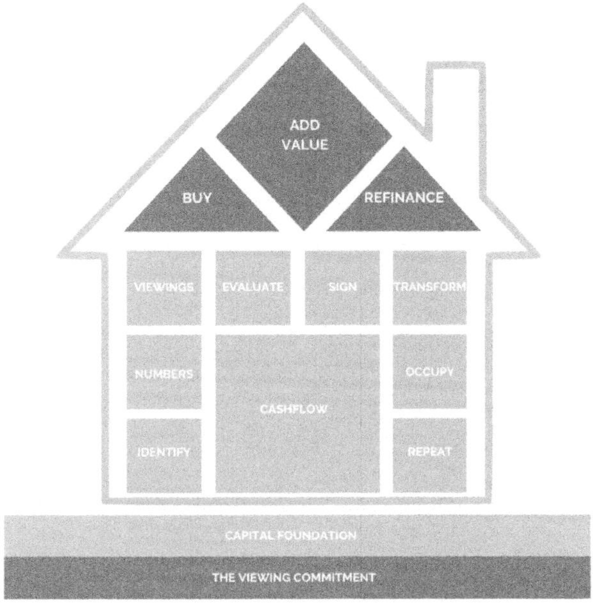

SUMMARY

We hope a few lightbulbs have come on when you read through the BAR method. It's an easy-to-understand process and we hope you will see the massive difference it could make to your investing journey. In fact, it's quite possible that this will shave decades off your hard work and supercharge it. People who don't understand this method never quite understand how others grow a portfolio or have the patience to wait for the right deal, and so they get stuck.

This process can help you grow your own portfolio, whether that is over 12 months or over the next decade; it depends on how much time you have and how much marketing you do to get the right deals. You can go as quickly or as slowly as you want. Buy a property well, add value and refinance in eight months or eight years' time if you wish, but the BAR method enables the process either way.

Remember that the combination of all three parts of BAR will give you infinitely greater returns than parking all your cash or deposits into the first house you find for sale.

CHAPTER 6

THE INVESTOR PROCESS™

The INVESTOR process is an eight-step process of all the things you need to do, in the right order.

I FOR IDENTIFY

There are two parts to identify:

1. **Identify your reason why. Motivation is great, but it can't be your only source of support when you need to keep going for a long time.**

2. **Identify your investing area.**

Why do you need a reason why?

Because motivation is not enough.

Improving yourself isn't always easy. It requires you to challenge yourself every day and work hard towards your big goal! Even though motivation can get you started, it can't always keep you going. At a certain point, motivation won't be enough to keep you going forward and reaching your goal.

In reality, having a 'reason why' is the only way to keep yourself going when you're facing difficulties along the way. It turns something that is abstract into something tangible and understandable. In other words, it gives meaning to what you are doing and helps you to remember why you started in the first place.

Here are five things you can do to keep motivation high:

1. **Learn to love 'no'; embrace rejection as a method of getting to success and a yes.**
2. **Take care of your body and mind.**
3. **Print out a vision board, making your 'reason why' powerful.**
4. **Tell everyone why you are doing property investing – it will keep you accountable.**
5. **Keep track of your progress, recognising how much you have learnt and how confident you are now – but remember not to just focus on your outcomes.**

How do you identify your investing area?

Call your agents in the area you're looking to invest in and simply ask them what they think the supply and demand levels are in those areas. You could also tell them you're looking to invest in the area and may need them to help you manage the property moving forward.

How to make sure there's a good demand:

1. **Choose an area where a lot of people want to live.**
2. **Choose an area where many people work and go to university.**
3. **Choose a spacious home (people like space).**
4. **Consider the aesthetics. Does it look nice? Is it well designed? Have you spent all the money on bricks and plaster, or can you add colour, interior design, etc.?**
5. **Create a good-quality product. Your property should be in a good area, with all the facilities you would expect and good access links and parking.**
6. **Improve your marketing – how effective are you at attracting lots of leads for tenants? The greater the demand, the lower the price pressure you will experience.**

Most investors invest in an area they live close to. Why? It is practical. I would always prefer to invest in an area where I had good market knowledge and understanding.

How to make sure you buy in an area where prices will rise:

- **Geek out on the statistics related to the property. Does the area command good rental rates? You can check this by looking online at sites such as spareroom.co.uk, and then compare the number of people looking for a room against the number of people selling rooms. What's the comparison? What are other investors doing, and how much are they selling their rooms for?**

- Find out whether it is a student area. If it is, then make sure that (if you choose students) the area isn't oversaturated. Call the university and check whether they have any plans to build more first-year halls, or if they are looking to take on any more properties.
- Find out if the area has any industry, such as local factories or blue-chip companies. You can market to the HR department directly and target people on the postgraduate scheme. Does the area have a hospital? HMOs close to hospitals are a great investment as they can be filled with young doctors, locums and nurses.
- Find out if the area is safe. We obviously have a duty to provide safe accommodation and we need to keep the houses populated, so a nice, secure safe area works better.
- Check out what local amenities there are. Is there a gym, supermarket etc. in the area? Location is always going to be key here; the closer to the train station and public transport links the property is, the better!

N FOR NUMBERS

Business is about numbers. Good business is about mastering numbers. It's getting your capital to work really hard and getting returns. It's making sure you have added enough value to return the capital borrowed to the investor.

We take a deep dive into the numbers, how to invest and what metrics to use. Some businesses have a loss-making model to start out with. For example, Amazon made huge losses in the first few years of trading but now it's a business giant. However, in property you need cash and capital to invest to start with and move into positive cashflow. Making a small loss each month means you will have to supplement your property investing from other sources – and therefore you cannot scale. We don't have big backers with huge pots of money, so we need to get a grasp of the money we need and the returns we are likely to get. How hard is your money working for you?

Everything comes together here.

Firstly, your capital situation and the availability of cash to invest is important. Is this your funds or is it someone else's money? How you invest and the risks you take are different. You may need to be more patient with an investor's funds, and you will need to work out how to refinance their cash to give it back to them. You will also need to talk to a broker about how you can use those funds, as already discussed.

Secondly, does the property cashflow? Does it make money each month?

This is where BAR comes in, and the three main factors are:

1. **How well did you buy? What price did you pay, and how much money do you have to pay each month in interest costs?**

2. **How much value can you add? How much value can you create to generate the maximum monthly rental? What is the maximum number of rooms and units and therefore cashflow? Will the refurbishment cost less than the increase in equity? In regard to the refurbishment, how much money will you spend to achieve the finished product?**

3. **What is the final refinance number?**

Then it's about how many of these deals you can find to grow and scale your portfolio as quickly as possible.

V FOR VIEWINGS

You should never buy a property without viewing it first. Viewings are, as we've already discussed, the key to getting property. The number of viewings you are doing will make a big difference to the amount of deals you do.

Build relationships with owners and agents. Have a chat. Relax and create rapport. Discover how to be seen as a credible buyer of property.

When you are on a viewing, you need to be methodical and go through a checklist. It's easy to get caught up in the emotion of buying a house and miss obvious stuff. When we moved house recently, it wasn't until we moved in that we realised the house had no heating in our son's bedroom! We had small fan heaters going for a few months until the plumber could fix us up a couple of radiators, which (when we added a full system flush) meant it cost us a further couple of thousand pounds. This house was our home and we'd approached the buying of it completely differently, and that was why we got caught out.

Please see the 'House Viewings' and 'Active Deals' sections of The Property Millionaire Planner. Check you know what they look like, so you are aware of them when carrying out viewings. The point here is to not become a surveyor but to at least have some frame of reference so you know when a deal might have too many challenges – or when there might be some issues that will frighten off other buyers but you know you can buy the property and fix the problems for a small fee.

Things to research:

- **Damp**
- **Rising damp**
- **Mould**
- **Mould due to condensation**
- **Wet rot**
- **Dry rot**
- **Asbestos in the home**
- **Cracking in brickwork**
- **Subsidence**
- **Concrete construction methods**

- **Timber-framed properties**
- **Flat roofs**

A good viewing is a viewing that takes into account all the items that need fixing and improving, so you can effectively cost the project once you are back at your desk.

Check covenants at this point as well. Covenants are restrictions on how the property can be used, that are placed on the Land Registry and the deeds of the property. You want to make sure you can use your property for its intended use. If the property has a covenant, then it is possible, but not guaranteed, that you could get it removed – but this could add significant cost to your purchase as you may have to negotiate with the beneficiary of the covenant. For example, some developers who sell a property may put a covenant on it to say that no new houses can be built. This can only be released if the beneficiary agrees, and it's likely to involve a substantial cost to obtain their permission. Other covenants restrict uses to residential, no shops, no brothels(!), no drinking establishments and so on.

A good viewing checks information like when appliances and heating systems were installed – are they approaching end of life? Will you need to cost in replacement in a few years. Is the roof new, or when was it last replaced? Typically, flat roofs have a life of 10–15 years and traditional clay tile roofs have a life of 50–100 years. Concrete tile roofs have a life of 40–75 years. Think about when the house was built and what life is left in the roof.

Room sizes and space are important to consider for HMOs and how you can get to the minimum space standards that your council has set. Look up your local amenities standards and print a copy and take it with you.

Make sure that you also check your local council housing and planning portal for any local policies that may affect your investment. You only need to do this once and then you are up to speed. If your council has a local development plan, this is also very useful. You will find out how to save your time and energy and work on projects that have a higher chance of success. It's not the most riveting of stuff but, if you are going to take property investment seriously, you should consider improving your local knowledge as a money-making activity.

If you've been through the above steps and are happy, then it's time to calculate what you can offer.

E FOR EVALUATE

Doing the numbers and due diligence is often the bit that drives us all to procrastination and overwhelm. If you are not getting deals agreed, then two things are happening:

1. **You don't have enough deals to evaluate and stack. They don't work, and you may be overanalysing them until you think they work. You think you are missing something when you are not. The deal is pants. It will never stack, no matter how much you keep running the numbers, tweaking the rent, lowering the costs. You are trying to make it work.**

2. **You haven't done enough hard work. There is a difference between understanding a deal doesn't work and having**

done none of the analysis. If you are unsure about a deal, ignoring the rent you can pay and the night rate you can charge is going to stop you from putting in an offer. Firstly, whenever you are unsure about the figures, such as rent, price and costs, you don't have anything to analyse. Get clear on what you can charge.

If you aren't any good with numbers, you may resist this section and go on in blind faith that you are doing the right thing. Your gut reaction may be as far as your due diligence goes. Property investing is very forgiving when you buy normal houses with three or four bedrooms. Generally, the main market has such strong supply and demand that, if you hold onto property for long enough, then any over-priced house you bought will be worth double what you bought it for. The most common mistake is buying a new build. Developers who are making a profit often price them at the top end of the market, so when you purchase a new house, you then fall into negative equity for a few years. A new house is attractive to buyers, as they don't need a budget for renovations and repairs; everything is already done for them.

When evaluating your leads, this is when you can assess whether the vendor might be open to doing something creative. If the vendor doesn't need the money, they may often be open to other strategies, such as renting it to you or agreeing to an option and selling it in a few years' time.

Planning permissions

Checking the property for the correct planning permissions is often a responsibility we delegate to our solicitor. However, you can quickly ascertain this by reviewing the planning portal to check to see if there is any planning permission. If it's not obvious, that is where it gets tricky. There are certificates you can go and obtain called Certificate of Lawful Existing Use or Development (CLEUD) notices. These are inexpensive when they are made during the buying process, requiring just a few hundred pounds and some help to establish the use. Post purchase, they are very expensive, where we are trying to obtain something critical to the hundreds of thousands of pounds we have just spent on the property. If in doubt, get a CLEUD – they are quick and have a time-bound decision process. You present your evidence, and the planning department has to produce counter-evidence if it does not agree with your presentation of evidence. This is normally quite tricky for a planning department to do. It also means that, during the buying process, you have the owner who is supporting your queries and requirements for proof of use. Once you have completed the sale, the owner is not obliged to continue to help, nor do they care what planning issues you are facing.

For the use: you must understand and know the use of the property and its history from the owner.

For extensions: check that any recent extensions match the house outline on the Land Registry. Has an extension been built under permitted development rules? Is this within the guidelines of what is allowed?

For annexes: is this a separate dwelling and therefore needs planning permission, or is it dependent on the main house? Does the extension itself need planning permission?

Survey: hopefully, when you viewed the property, you will have spotted any concerning issues. You can instruct a survey to make sure you are buying a good property and get an expert to address any issue or concerns you have since the viewing.

If at any point your due diligence starts to spot potential problems, you can renegotiate the price with your vendor.

Try and go at some pace during this process, as you need to learn to make decisions quickly. You can be looking for a property forever while others are purchasing, renovating and then cashflowing their property. Procrastination can cost you dearly.

If we are going to work out the value of the property relative to the market, then we need to make sure we are paying the right price for the house and area. The first thing we're going to do is open up one of the property portals and go through a desktop analysis of deals:

1. **Search for the property you are looking to buy/stack and enter the general search location.**

2. **Sort properties in ascending price. What do you notice about the prices in the area compared with the deal you are stacking? Things that affect price include proximity to roads, parking, local amenities and local undesirable amenities (e.g., a nightclub next door).**

3. **Estimate the price of the property after you have added value and refurbished it.**

To put in an offer, we need to understand what all the purchase costs are. They include:

1. **The purchase price**
2. **Legals**
3. **Stamp duty**
4. **Refurbishment**
5. **HMO licence fee (licences are not transferable)**
6. **Valuation fee**
7. **Broker fee**
8. **% Deposit**

Having got all this information together, you now realise how much cash you'll need to buy the property.

Next, look at the ROI figure – how hard is your money working? If you are refinancing, you can also work this out based on the residual investment left in. If all your money is pulled back out on refinancing, this will be an infinite return.

Next, calculate the mortgage at your interest rate.

For an HMO, we calculate the bills. For serviced accommodation, we need to calculate laundry and cleaning costs.

Calculate the cashflow per month.

Calculate the cashflow per annum.

If we are happy that this looks reasonable, we proceed to legals.

S FOR SIGN

The 'sign' that you have a great business is the ability of that business to scale and grow. If you have a one-hit wonder, then there is generally not enough income to keep you or your business going. Businesses need cash to survive. I don't mean 'to support you', either; a limited company needs a set of accounts producing each year, it needs to pay for a bank account, website fees, a telephone system. A software fee for basic business tools like spreadsheets or accounting systems. These few things alone can add up to £200 per month. And that's before the doors are open.

If you are to scale, you need to do things in a way that is legal and legally binding. You need to follow proper due diligence, with contractually sound and clear responsibilities, as all of that will give strength to your business.

Whatever strategy you follow – and that includes rent-to-rents, purchase lease options, leasehold, joint ventures, assisted sales, investor finance, mortgages and purchases – using a solicitor or lawyer is not just for a purchase. Remember that we talked about how the whole house-buying process in the UK is covered by the Land Registry. Your property is protected by this system, and this also makes home buying a strong strategy for banks and financiers to be sure that a) the asset exists and b) there are no other interested parties on the register or that Land Registry will insure their exposure.

We can't think of one scenario where you don't want to get a lawyer involved. The challenge is to find a lawyer who understands and is helpful in what you are trying to achieve, particularly with more creative strategies. Sometimes solicitors can be the deal-prevention police.

Even where family or friends are involved, a lifetime of friendship can be destroyed over £1,000. You must, must, *must* get a lawyer involved to protect those relationships. Draw up a simple one-page loan or joint-venture agreement so that, should you need to, you will have a document as reference. The beauty of a document is that it can be pulled out of the cupboard quietly, so people can check back their understanding. They may never mention anything to you, but it will prevent any misunderstanding or disagreements.

Get things done properly, and the legals will protect you and your future interests.

T FOR TRANSFORM

Refurbishing a property can create massive value, but it's important to consider what is in a brand and what style you're going for. A brand should be timeless and have staying power. For example, if you're targeting millennials, you might want to consider a more modern style. If you're targeting baby boomers, you might want to go for a more classic look. If the property is being marketed as a luxury development, then using high-end materials and finishes will be essential in order to create the desired perception. However, if the property is being marketed as more of a budget-friendly option, then using lower-cost materials may be more appropriate.

When it comes to creating a luxurious finish in a property, one of the key elements is choosing the right colours. Bold and eye-catching colours can help to create a feeling of luxury, while more subdued tones can add an air of sophistication.

Here are some tips for choosing colours that will create a luxurious finish in your property:

- **Go for bold and bright colours. Rich jewel tones are always luxurious, as are bright and vibrant shades. If you want to make a statement, choose colours that will really stand out.**
- **Consider using metallics. Gold, silver and bronze can add a touch of glamour to any space. In fact, metallics can be used as accents very effectively.**

Your property is an important investment, and you want to make sure it is well maintained and looks its best. A luxury finish can help you command higher rents, giving you a better return on your investment. If you are looking to give your property an edge in the rental market, then a luxury finish is definitely worth considering.

Vanilla and magnolia are perhaps the two most popular paint colours for walls. They are safe, inoffensive choices that go with almost any decorating style. However, when refurbishing a property, it is important to steer clear of these two colours. The reason is simple: they are incredibly boring. A property that has been freshly painted in vanilla or magnolia is unlikely to stand out from the crowd. In a competitive market, it is essential to make a property as appealing as possible. This means creating a space that is both stylish and unique. While vanilla and magnolia might be popular choices, they are not likely to help a property stand out from the competition.

In a competitive market, interior design can be the secret ingredient that sets your property apart from the rest. In addition, a well-designed space will be more attractive to prospective tenants, helping you fill units quickly. With so much on the line, it's clear that interior design is an important tool for any property owner or manager.

A quick word on safety. You should always work in your business with your employees' and contractors' safety in mind. In the UK we have the CDM regulations from 2015 that are a set of guidelines that govern the construction process. The regulations aim to improve health and safety standards in the construction industry by ensuring that all workers are properly trained and have the necessary equipment to carry out their work safely. The regulations also set out clear responsibilities for those in charge of construction projects, so that everyone knows who is responsible for what. By following the CDM regulations, construction companies can help to prevent accidents and injuries, and ensure that their projects are completed on time and to a high standard. This is you, if you are refurbishing a property and using more than one trade or your contractor uses more than one subcontractor, including the plumber, the plasterer, the electrician and so on.

You must also consider asbestos. Asbestos is a dangerous material that can cause serious health problems if it is not properly managed. If you own a property that contains asbestos, it is important to take the necessary steps to protect yourself and others from exposure. First, you should have the property inspected by a qualified professional who can identify where the asbestos is located and what condition it is in. Once the asbestos has been located, you will need to take steps to seal or remove it. If the asbestos is in good condition and well sealed, you may be able to leave it in place. However, if the asbestos is damaged or not properly sealed, it will need to be removed by a trained professional. Taking these steps will help to ensure that your property is safe and free from potential hazards.

By carefully planning and sticking to a budget, you can ensure that your project will be completed on time and within your desired budget. In addition, by doing your research and shopping around for the best deals, you can save even more money.

After the refurb has finished and you are selling or renting a property, it is important to present it in the best possible light. This process, known as staging, can help to make a property more attractive to potential buyers or tenants. Staging can help to create a positive first impression and maximise the value of the property. In addition, staging can also help to make a property more marketable by highlighting its best features. As

“

Your property is an important investment, and you want to make sure it is well maintained and looks its best.

”

a result, even properties that are not in perfect condition can benefit from staging. Ultimately, staging is an effective way to increase the chances of selling or renting a property quickly and at a fair price.

O FOR OCCUPY

Often people won't even entertain getting into property because they have heard horror stories about tenants trashing a landlord's home. In reality, this happens very rarely, and the higher the quality of the house, the better the tenants you get, which means the less chance you have of them abusing the property. You can always use deposits and ensure you have a way to collect any costs of repairs. In reality, while any messy or dirty property or damages may look horrendous, they often appear a lot worse than they actually are, and it doesn't take long to bring a property back up to standard. A professional carpet clean, a repaint and replacing a few items can soon get your property back on the market and cost you less than a few thousand pounds.

Even so, the key is to get the *right* tenants from day one, but the fear over this means it's not uncommon for new landlords to be a little scared at first. Just do one thing at a time - and trust yourself to get great tenants on board.

You want to make sure that you are getting someone who is going to take care of your property and pay their rent on time. You may consider using an agent, but this might be costly for what you need.

There are a few things you can do to make sure you are finding the best tenants possible:

- **Check their credit score. One of the best ways to get an idea of how responsible a potential tenant is can be to get them referenced. You can use companies like Letting Ref.**
- **Always ask for references. You should especially focus on the previous landlord, not just on their current landlord. They may want to get rid of their tenant and could give a good reference, even though that is illegal. The previous landlord will be the most honest and graphic in describing your tenant.**
- **Google your tenant's name and town. You'd be surprised at what people post on social media about themselves; references to drug smoking and party photos are clues as to how a potential tenant may use your property. Any newspaper articles about them perhaps committing criminal activity are also going to show you what to expect.**
- **Get landlord insurance. It's possible to get insurance to cover your rent and any eviction procedures; just google landlord insurance. Make sure you do this before getting the tenant, as the insurers will probably vet the applicant with you.**
- **Get your tenant on the right documentation. This is called an Assured Shorthold Tenancy, and you need to ensure your house is compliant. You can use landlord management software for self-managing property, like our software**

GO Tenant, which will help you recruit and issue the right documents to tenants and comply with housing legislation. We offer a free 28-day trial.

Collecting the rent is the bit you started this all for. This is the reward for investing in property. Don't forget you are providing someone with a home, and this is truly a win–win scenario, when you can help someone who needs a home to live in.

R FOR REPEAT

There is no one-size-fits-all answer to the question of how to scale a property portfolio business. However, there are a few key factors that can help ensure success as your company grows. First and foremost, it is important to have a clear vision for your business and a detailed plan for how to achieve your goals.

In business, as in life, it is important to identify what works well and then keep doing it. This may seem obvious, but it can be difficult to maintain focus when there are always new challenges and opportunities arising. One way to stay on track is to establish a set of core values that guide all your decision-making. These values should be based on what has proven to be successful in the past. Once they are in place, it will be easier to stay focused on what is important and ignore distractions.

Another key element is to establish clear goals, objectives and what you want to do when you have achieved them. Having a roadmap in place will help you to make decisions and keep going.

A positive mindset is essential for achieving success in any endeavour. When you believe in yourself and your ability to succeed, you are more likely to take risks and persevere through challenges. On the other hand, a negative mindset can quickly lead to self-doubt and defeat.

In addition to cultivating a positive mindset, it is also important to surround yourself with like-minded people. This is because our beliefs and attitudes are often shaped by those around us. If we constantly associate with people who are negative and pessimistic, it will be difficult to maintain a positive outlook on life. You are unlikely to repeat a negative experience over and over again. A learning mindset is important when growing a property business.

Therefore, it is important to cultivate a positive mindset. Property can be lonely, if you are making lots of decisions every day and have no one to share your worries and concerns with. Seeking out fellow investors to work with will really help.

Focus on your strengths and play to them. There is no point in trying to be good at everything; it is better to identify the things you do well and make sure you do them better than anyone else. It is also important to always be learning and adapting to the ever-changing business landscape. Keeping up with new trends and technologies will help you to stay ahead of the competition and keep your business relevant.

Why should you run your property business rather than setting and forgetting it?

One of the biggest mistakes property investors make is thinking that their portfolio will run itself. They purchase a property, put it with an agent and then forget about it until it's time to renew the lease or make repairs. However, this hands-off approach can lead to a number of problems. Even if you are using an agent, you need to monitor and check their performance. If you had an employee, you'd expect to regularly check in with them and monitor their work. Just because it is an agent, it does not mean they are always going to be doing the right things or carrying out all of their duties. It is still your job to check up on them.

Any business, no matter how big or small, needs to have a handle on its finances. This is especially true for property businesses, which often involve large sums of money and complex transactions. There are a few key things you can do to help keep your property business's finances under control. Firstly, make sure to keep accurate records of all income and expenses. This will give you a clear picture of where your money is coming from and where it is going to, and it will help you to identify any areas where you may be overspending. Secondly, create a budget for your business and stick to it as much as possible. This will help you to allocate your funds in a deliberate way and prevent you from overspending. Finally, work with a qualified accountant, outsourcing your bookkeeping and accounting to a professional service. This way, you can focus on other aspects of your business and leave the financials to someone else. After all, unless you are qualified, it is difficult to stay on top of tax legislation and changes.

Any business should be reviewed and updated regularly, and a property business is no different. By taking an active role in running your property business, you can ensure that it continues to meet your needs and achieve your goals.

It is important to keep looking for properties and marketing for your business (check out Rick's book *45 Ways to Find Property* for ideas about marketing), even when you are busy. Marketing helps to create awareness, so when a potential seller hears your name, they will think of you first. As you are scaling and growing your property business, you will want more property leads to go and view. This means that, when the time is ready, you can *repeat*, go back to the beginning and start again.

SUMMARY

So, there you have the eight-step process:

- **I for identify**
- **N for numbers**
- **V for viewings**
- **E for evaluate**
- **S for sign**
- **T for transform**
- **O for occupy**
- **R for repeat**

Lorraine remembers starting out in her new procurement business. Having been an accountant for 20 years, she found it overwhelming at times because it was completely new.

She says, 'The only way I could explain how I felt was that, at each stage, I kept doing the next thing and then the next thing, and once I had completed something, I felt relieved for 60 seconds, and then I realised (and panicked) about how much I didn't know for what I needed to do next. At first, it was to learn how to sell to a new customer, then it was to get the customer to sign up with me, then I had to deliver the work and then I had to invoice them and hope they would pay me! Property investing is similar to this. I would have become overwhelmed and stopped if I had thought about it all, but I just trusted at each stage that I would figure it out with help.'

The eight steps are laid out in order and, if followed, will help you to move through the process in a logical and methodical way. Everyone thinks they know how to do this stuff, until they start. Trust the process. Property is a lot about detail – and details matter, but not all at once. The eight steps are great ways to think about how to get the best out of your property investing. A journey of a thousand miles starts with a single step.

CHAPTER 7

THE IMPORTANCE OF TIME AND MONEY

HOW QUICKLY CAN YOU BECOME A PROPERTY MILLIONAIRE?

The old saying goes, 'if you want something done, ask a busy person'. And there's a lot of truth to that. Busy people tend to be more organised and efficient with their time. They know how to prioritise and get things done quickly. They're also usually pretty good at delegating tasks. So, if you've got a task that needs to be done, it's often best to ask a busy person to do it – and that busy person might be you. Stop telling yourself that you are too busy, as that is self-sabotage. You are likely to get it done more quickly and efficiently than you think. And always look for someone else who can help you get it done.

If you're like most people, you probably have a lot on your plate. Between work, family and social obligations, it can be tough to find time for anything else. So, when you're faced with a new project, it can be hard to know where to start. The key is to prioritise.

First, take a look at the project and decide what needs to be done. Make a list of all the tasks involved, big and small. Then you can start assigning priorities. What needs to be done first? What can wait? And what can be delegated to someone else? This may seem like a daunting task, but if you break it down into smaller steps, you'll be able to handle it. We think it's really important to agree with partners and family, understanding that you won't be able to do all the things you normally do. You might need to agree that the lounge won't get painted this year. It's just not on the list any more. Explain to them the dream you have and what you want to achieve with property investing. You can promise your partner a holiday of a lifetime.

When it comes to achieving our goals, confidence is key. After all, if we don't believe in ourselves, how can we expect others to believe in us? But what exactly is confidence? And how can we cultivate it? Confidence is basically a feeling of trust in our own abilities. It's the belief that we can handle whatever comes our way and that we have what it takes to succeed. This doesn't mean that we're always sure of ourselves – everyone has moments of doubt. But confident people are able to brush off these doubts and keep moving forward.

So, how can we become more confident? One way is to focus on our successes, rather than our failures. Every time we accomplish something, no matter how small, we're building up our confidence, so make sure you keep a check on how much you are achieving, even if this is ruling out property and deals that don't work.

The more trust you place in your ability to learn what you need to know, to make the right decision when needed, the more progress you will make. So, next time you're struggling to get going, remember that the key is simply to keep moving forward. The confidence will come, and when it does, you'll be astonished at what you can achieve.

KEEP GOING

It's not all plain sailing; at times you will want to give up. You will discover new things about the property and about the property market. You may want to change your offer or renegotiate to ensure the deal still works for you.

Any good deal has three key ingredients:

1. **Understanding what the other person wants**
2. **Finding common ground**
3. **Being willing to compromise**

When it comes to making a difficult deal happen, those three elements are even more important.

The first step is to take the time to really understand the other person's position. What are their goals? What are their concerns?

The more trust you place in your ability to learn what you need to know, to make the right decision when needed, the more progress you will make.

What are they willing to budge on? Once you have a clear sense of their objectives, you can start to look for points of agreement.

Even if the overall deal is very complicated, there are likely to be some basic principles that both sides can agree on. But be prepared to give a little bit. No one gets everything they want in a deal, and your being willing to give up something is likely to ensure the deal stays on the table.

It's not uncommon for a property deal to get complicated. There can be a lot of moving parts, and it's easy to get bogged down in the details. However, it's important to keep moving forward, even when the going gets tough.

Here are a few tips to help you stay on track:

1. **Make sure you have a clear understanding of your goal and then move one tiny step forward each and every day. It doesn't matter how small, but if you can move the project forward or even backward, this is healthier than being stuck.**

2. **Stay organised and keep track of all the details. This will help you to identify any potential roadblocks and find solutions more quickly.**

3. **Communicate with all the professionals and stakeholders and keep them up to date. We regularly phone agents and tell them surveys have been done or even booked. To the other side, this is progress, and it builds confidence that the deal is going ahead.**

4. **Don't be afraid to ask for help or for further clarifications and explanations, if you're feeling overwhelmed.**

5. **Details matter in complex and difficult deals. Don't kid yourself they don't. They crop up two days before completion and the underwriting department wants to check something before they release the funds. This is a particularly stressful time. Get people to confirm in writing that they have grasped the point you are clarifying.**

Sometimes, when we're feeling exhausted or just plain done on a deal, all we need is to push ourselves to do one more thing, whether it's completing the next task, making the next phone call or replying to yet another query from the bank. Keep going.

If your brain is overwhelmed, go for a run, walk the dogs, read a book or have a bath. That tiny step away will give you the energy and time to complete that one extra task that could shatter the glass ceiling.

Just breathe. The stress response in the body can be triggered by difficult conversations, and you slip into defensive mode. But being defensive doesn't help you get a difficult deal done. If your stress levels are rising, do some deep breathing exercises to switch off that stress; you are not fighting a sabre-toothed tiger, it's not life or death. Try to stay calm.

While it may not seem like much in the moment, that one extra thing can make all the difference in the long run. So, next time you're feeling like you can't go on, just try to do one more thing.

Good diary habits can help make your business more successful. By keeping a record of your daily activities, you can more easily see what works and what doesn't, identify areas that need improvement, and track your progress over time.

LEGACY AND PASSING ON WEALTH IN TIME

You want to leave a lasting legacy for your loved ones. We hope you can see how creating a property portfolio will provide your family with a steady income for years to come, and it will also help to create and preserve your wealth.

For many people, retirement planning is all about finding the right balance between security and flexibility. And for some, that means choosing a property portfolio over a traditional pension fund.

Here are just a few of the benefits that come with owning a property portfolio:

- **You have more control over how your money is invested. With a pension fund, you're at the mercy of the fund managers. But with a property portfolio, you can make your own investment decisions and choose where to invest your money. With a pension fund, you are stuck with the stock market and other factors that are beyond your control.**

- **Your investment is more tangible. When you invest in a pension fund, your money goes into a pot that's managed by someone else. But when you invest in property, you're**

buying something that you can see and touch. This makes it easier to keep track of your investment and see how it's performing.

- **A property portfolio can be passed on – or at least, the wealth can. An annuity can't be passed on; it dies with the beneficiary.**

When it comes to property investing, there are many different ways to approach it. Some people choose to go it alone, while others prefer to work with a financial adviser to help them plan their portfolio. If you're thinking about leaving your property portfolio to your family, it's important to do some planning ahead of time. Working with a financial adviser can help you to figure out the best way to structure your portfolio so that your family can benefit from it in the future. They can also offer guidance on how to manage and grow your portfolio so that it continues to provide value for your family after you're gone. With a little planning and forethought, you can ensure that your property portfolio leaves a lasting impact on your loved ones.

It's never too early to start planning for retirement. By thinking ahead and making some smart choices, you can ensure that you'll have the financial resources you need to enjoy a comfortable retirement. One of the first things to consider is when you'd like to retire. This will help you determine how much you'll need to save each year. If you want to retire at 65, for example, you'll need to save enough money to cover about 20 years of expenses. In addition to thinking about when you'd like to retire, it's also important to consider how much money you'll need to support your lifestyle. Do you want to travel? Make a major purchase? Be able to help your children or grandchildren with their education? The more specific you are about your retirement goals, the easier it will be to create a plan that will help you reach them.

You'll want to think about what kind of property you'll need to live in and how you'll maintain it once you're no longer working. Do you want a large piece of land with a big house, or would you prefer a smaller home that's easier to take care of? Consider your lifestyle and needs when making your decision. If you plan on travelling or spending more time at your second home, for example, you'll want to make sure that your primary residence is low maintenance. Whatever you decide, it's important to have a plan in place so that you can enjoy your retirement years without worrying about your property.

It's also important to think about how your buy-to-let properties and portfolio will fit into your plans. If you're looking to downsize, you may want to sell up and release some equity and possibly restructure to prioritise that.

- **Easy to maintain - perhaps they are newer**
- **In an area with good rental demand**
- **Attract long-term tenants**
- **Are simpler designs**
- **Are easy to access**
- **Provide significant income (cherry-pick the best ones)**

A property portfolio can provide you with a solid foundation for retirement, and there are many different ways to go about building one.

£10 MILLION PROPERTY INVESTOR

Reaching a property portfolio worth £10 million in 10 years may seem impossible, but with careful planning and execution, it can be done. If we are talking house prices of £250k plus, it's just 40 houses. That's four houses per annum. Ten years.

Here are our five best tips to help you on your way:

Have a clear goal and a plan of action

Developing a clear goal is the first step on the road to building a £10 million property portfolio. Without a destination in mind, it can be all too easy to veer off course. By setting a target of 10 years and £10 million, you can create a roadmap for your journey and track your progress along the way. Of course, reaching such a lofty goal will require more than just wishful thinking. In addition to setting a clear goal, you'll need to develop a comprehensive plan of action. This should include strategies for acquiring properties, managing your finances, and building your portfolio over time. With careful planning and execution, it is possible to achieve remarkable success in the world of property investing.

Stay disciplined and invest regularly

If you are to create a £10 million property portfolio, then you should stay disciplined and invest regularly. This may seem like common sense, but it's important to remember that property investing is a long-term game. While there will be ups and downs along the way, the key is to stay the course and keep investing consistently. Of course, this doesn't mean that you should blindly invest in any property that comes your way. Doing your research and being selective about your investments is still essential.

It's not always easy to stick to a plan or a routine, but if you can be disciplined and stick with it, you'll be much more likely to reach your goal. Find someone who has already achieved what you're trying to do and ask them for advice.

The relationship between discipline and freedom is a complex one. On the one hand, discipline is often seen as the enemy of freedom, with strict rules and regulations constraining our ability to act. On the other hand, discipline can also be seen as the foundation of freedom, providing the structure and stability that allow us to pursue our goals. In reality, the two are interconnected, and neither can exist without the other. Freedom without discipline quickly degenerates into chaos, while discipline without freedom stifles creativity and eventually leads to stagnation. Only by striking a balance between the two can we hope to achieve our full potential as individuals.

Do your research and find the right properties

The UK property market has been through some tough times in recent years, but there are still opportunities out there for savvy investors. Look for areas that are undergoing regeneration or where new infrastructure is being built, as these areas are likely to see an increase in property values. It's also important to be realistic about your budget and targets. Don't try to stretch yourself too thin by buying too many properties; it's better to focus on quality over quantity. With the right approach, it is possible to build a £10 million portfolio within 10 years.

Be patient – Rome wasn't built in a day!

One of the most important pieces of advice for anyone looking to build a property portfolio is to be patient. Rome wasn't built in a day, and neither will your £10 million portfolio be. Don't make the wrong decisions; just keep progressing sensibly. Patience is key. Just do one more thing to find and get the properties.

Keep learning and growing as an investor

The most important tip for anyone looking to create a £10 million property portfolio in 10 years is to keep learning and growing as an investor. The world of property investing is always changing, and those who are able to adapt and evolve will be the most successful. There are a number of ways to stay ahead of the game, such as reading industry publications, attending conferences and networking with other investors. By continually expanding your knowledge base, you'll be in a much better position to make wise investment decisions that can lead to immense wealth.

Reaching a £10 million property portfolio is an ambitious goal, but it's certainly achievable with the right approach. By staying disciplined and investing regularly, doing your research, being patient and continuing to learn and grow as an investor, you'll be well on your way to creating serious wealth through property. So don't give up – keep reaching for the stars!

DOES MONEY GO TO MONEY?

Money is one of the most important things in life. It can provide security and comfort, and it can help you achieve your goals. But where does the money come from? And where does it go? What is the truth about wealth distribution?

What is money and where does it come from?

Many people believe that money is simply a medium of exchange, a way to buy goods and services. However, money is much more than that. Money is actually an idea. It is a unit of measurement that we use to quantify the value of goods and services. We use money because it is easier than bartering for goods and services. For example, if I want to buy a new car, I do not have to find someone who has a car and wants my house. I can simply go to a dealership and trade my money for a car.

Where does money come from? Money is created when a government prints it or when a bank loans it into existence. When the government creates money, it is actually created when debt is incurred. When a government or business borrows money, the amount borrowed is created out of thin air and added to the economy. This can lead to inflation, as too much money chasing too few goods can drive up prices. In addition, the creation of money is not evenly distributed. The lion's share of money created goes to those who are already wealthy, as they are the ones who are able to borrow the most money. This results in a vicious cycle, as the rich get richer and the poor get poorer.

The flow of money through our economy

It's well known that the rich are getting richer while the poor are getting poorer. But what's driving this trend? One theory is that money simply flows to money. In other words, those who have money are more likely to see their wealth grow, while those who don't have much money will find it harder and harder to get ahead.

There's some evidence to support this theory. For example, studies have shown that the wealthy are more likely to invest their money, while the poor are more likely to save it. This means that the rich are able to take advantage of compound interest, while the poor are not. As a result, the gap between the rich and the poor is only likely to grow over time. Of course, there are other unfortunate factors at play as well, including inequalities based on education, race and gender.

Wealth, like water, follows the path of least resistance. Just as water will always travel downhill, money will always flow towards those who already have money. This simple truth helps to explain why the rich tend to get richer while the poor tend to stay poor. The flow of money through our economy is dictated by a series of complex financial laws, but the basic principle is straightforward: those who have money are more likely to receive even more money. There are several reasons why this is the case. As already identified, the rich are more likely to invest their money, but they also have more of it to begin with. Those who have money are more likely to invest it wisely and earn a healthier return on their investment. They can also afford to hire financial advisers, and people in their network are all likely to introduce them to ways to make even more money. And because they have more money, they are also more likely to be able to borrow more money (remember we talked about the power of leverage). This allows them to buy more and more assets, such as property or businesses, which in turn generate more money. It's brilliantly simple, really. Rather than despise the system or feel left out, we want to encourage and inspire you, so that you can benefit too. Property is a brilliant way to get on board with your very own 'get rich slow' plan.

The rich often inherit their wealth, and any self-made millionaires are keen to protect that wealth for future generations. They can give sizeable inheritances to their children or grandchildren, which gives them a leg up on the competition. In short, money begets money.

A recent study by the Equality Trust found that the richest 10% of households in the UK own 44% of the total wealth, while the poorest 50% own just 9%.[20] This inequality is even more pronounced when it comes to income, with the top 10% earning 56% of all income while the bottom 50% earn just 16%. The implications of these disparities are far-reaching and have a major impact on individuals and businesses alike.

There is wealth out there for everyone if you know where to look for it. Get a copy of the Property Millionaire Planner to really accelerate your success, maintaining a step-by-step planner that you fill out as you go.

Here are some tips on how to get your share of the wealth:

- **Look for opportunities to create value.**
- **Invest in yourself by taking courses and learning new skills.**
- **Start your own business and become self-employed.**
- **Network with people who can help you achieve your goals.**
- **Be patient - wealth doesn't come overnight.**
- **Stay positive and believe in yourself.**
- **Don't give up when things get tough.**

Whether it's starting a business, investing in property or simply finding a better-paid job, look for ways to increase your earnings. The more value you create, the more wealth you will earn. You are reading this book, and we believe that property is not only the best way to start but it is also the best asset class, because of the security that the Land Registry gives it and the opportunity you have to be able to leverage 75–85% of the property with financial lenders.

TOO BUSY

Do you feel like you've been saying that you'll start your new project 'next year' for the past 10 years? If so, you're not alone. Many people never find the time to do what they want because they are too busy with other things. However, it's important to remember that time never comes back, and the perfect time never arrives.

We all have the same 24 hours in a day, but it always seems like there's never enough time to get everything done. If you're feeling like the years are slipping away and you're not accomplishing everything you want to, it might be time to reassess your priorities and find ways to make more time for the things that are most important to you.

Take a close look at your list of priorities and figure out what can be moved to the bottom or removed entirely. Sometimes we can get caught up in non-essential tasks that add stress to our lives without actually moving us closer to our goals. By paring down your list, you can free up more time for the things that truly matter. Write a list of stuff that is not important (e.g., painting your lounge). Another way to make more time for your goals is to find ways to optimise the time you already have. For example, can you wake up a bit earlier in the morning so that you have more time to work on your goals?

Time has a way of slipping away, especially as we get older. Suddenly, it feels like 10 years have gone by in the blink of an eye. If you want to make the most of the next 10 years, there are some simple things you can do to help make that happen. Firstly, take some time to figure out what you want to accomplish in the next 10 years. What are your goals and dreams? Make a list. Once you have a good idea of what you want to achieve, start doing one small thing every day that will move you closer to your goal. It doesn't have to be anything big or fancy, just something that gets you one step closer. Don't worry about the full step-by-step sequence; just do the next thing to move towards the goal you want to achieve over the next 10 years.

Regrets are the worst type of emotion. You had the idea, you had the timing – but with zero action.

SNOWBALL EFFECT

The 'snowball effect' is a term that is used to describe how small investments can lead to big returns over time. When it comes to starting a property-investing business, this effect can be very powerful. Many people think they need a large amount of money to get started in this type of business, but this is simply not the case. With a small amount of money and some patience, it is possible to create a very successful property-investing business. The key to making the snowball effect work for you is to start small and focus on the deals that will allow you to momentum invest. By following this approach, you can create a property empire that will continue to grow and thrive for years to come. Remember to start small and reinvest the profits back into the business. This will allow you to gradually increase your investment portfolio and eventually reap the rewards of your hard work.

Clearly define your goals.

What do you hope to achieve by starting a property-investing business?

Do you want to generate income, build equity, or both?

Once you know what you want to accomplish, you can develop a strategy for achieving those goals.

Do your research. Before making any decisions, it's crucial to educate yourself about the ins and outs of property investing.

There are a lot of things to think about when starting a property-investing business. But don't let that overwhelm you! The most important thing is to start taking action. The sooner you get started, the sooner you'll start seeing results. And once you see results, it will be easier to stay motivated and keep going.

SUMMARY

Property investment is one of the smartest things you can do for your long-term financial security. While there's no magic formula for picking the perfect time to invest, there are certain factors that can help you to make a decision.

Many people wait until they feel confident about the market or have a large sum of money saved up before making their first investment, but this can often be a mistake. Property values can rise and fall very quickly, so waiting to invest could mean missing out on a great opportunity and capital growth. If you're thinking about investing in property, it's important to do your research and get into the market as soon as possible. Don't wait for the perfect moment – there may not be one. If you are holding for the long term and investing for cashflow, then it doesn't really matter if prices go up or down. It may stall your progress if you can't refinance your capital back out.

CHAPTER 8

WHEN WILL YOU TAKE YOUR FIRST STEP INTO PROPERTY INVESTING?

At some point, every successful property investor was in love with the idea of property, although they owned no properties. Full of potential, convinced property was the ideal vehicle to transform their personal wealth, they loved property from afar. At some point something hit them – a personal tragedy or a wakeup call on their own health – and then they realised they had been caught in the trap of 'time for money'. Selling your time for money offers you a perception of stability and security. However, you realise your security is based on the business success of someone else. When you have the clarity that you are selling your time for money, the hate for it compounds. It becomes a chore and seriously uncomfortable. The whole thing becomes a prickly cone that you have to hug up to each and every day. Once the pain of staying the same surpasses the pain of change, those successful property investors take the leap of faith.

You can do nothing, staying the same, and you may well forget the concepts in this book, forget the book and the ideas that could transform your wealth. You can sit in your home, meet the same people every day and wonder what if...? You sit on your couch all comfy today, but some day your life will be deteriorating, and the most common regret of the dying is the regret of not taking the chances and opportunities that life gave them.

This book is that wakeup call.

It's your opportunity.

It's your chance to make a few mistakes.

We deliberately say 'mistakes.' Why? Because you will make a tonne of them. You will regret the shade of green (Parakeet Blush) you chose for the lounge in your holiday let – it was too safe, you wish you'd used a bolder colour scheme. You will regret buying the cheaper bed frames for your HMOs, although your budget at the time wouldn't allow anything grander.

You will regret letting a tenant take a room that you had some doubts about.

But these are all *good* and great mistakes.

You will learn.

You won't make the same mistakes twice.

You won't regret investing in property.

WIN YOUR FINANCIAL FREEDOM

Know your current capital and cashflow position. What can you afford? How do you start? This is the foundation, as this is where you are starting from.

Learn the BAR Principles, and how to spot the opportunities in deals on the market.

Apply BAR to all of your deals, don't just spend your money.

Learn to invest it. Invest your investor-lent funds, so that you can pay them back.

Learn to find the right deal.

Not the desperate deal.

Learn how to create value in your property portfolio.

Anticipate that to scale and grow, you will need to refinance, that you will need to take your initial risk capital back out of the property to buy more.

Go through the INVESTOR steps. Your aim is to buy one property per quarter – four per year.

Make the viewing commitment. Do two viewings each and every week.

Do the hard work now that will save you from working hard all your life.

If you have ever wondered how people have 10-plus properties in their portfolios, and how they got all the funds, then this book should have been the eye-opener, and we're afraid you can't unknow this. Now your eyes are wide open. That means, our dear readers, you will never be able to ask that question again: 'but how do they do it?' You know.

So the question is really: when will you do this?

YOUR WEALTHY FUTURE

You now have the blueprint to not only replace your income through property investing but also to create and improve your wealth for you and generations to come. You can own a million pounds' worth of property, meaning you can scale to a million pounds' worth of equity.

We're excited for you.

It will be bloody hard work.

There will be days when you know you deserve success but it's not quite landed yet.

Hold steady.

Never give up.

Some people have beginner's luck, and it works quickly and effectively for them.

But trust in you. Invest in you. Do this for you. Even if it takes too long and it doesn't work for you straight away, hang in there.

Lorraine was recently ill with appendicitis. Approximately 10% of the population have appendicitis at some point, but it was a shock. But she sat on our couch at home and recuperated for six weeks. Our business meant that she could. There was no

“

There will be days when you know you deserve success but it’s not quite landed yet. Hold steady. Never give up.

”

pressure to get back to work. We didn't make any less money because of property investing.

At some point something will happen in your life that will mean you will want to get back your time. You can guarantee it will happen.

We often hear from people who are on final-salary pension schemes. They are staying in their jobs to reach retirement and receive a salary that is 40% of their working salary. This doesn't appear to be the deal of the century to us, nor worth staying in a job you hate for the next 20 years. But we get it.

Somehow worse is that you have money in the bank but you are somehow too scared to act. That money is not growing or earning income. You could be growing your wealth and cashflowing too.

Life's too short.

Believe us – there is another way to live.

Property can create a relatively passive income or (probably a more accurate way look at it) it can be leveraged as a possible income. Some days you will need to be involved; Rick currently works on the first day of the month, checking rents coming into the bank account.

Believe in property as a wealth-generation technique. If you bought your own home 20 years ago, then you know that property prices increase. You have probably seen a quadrupling of the value of your property, first hand.

If you ever had single lets or flipped a few properties for profit, then you will know that this is no strategy for long-term income or wealth generation. Choose high cashflow.

We know you want to make money without spending all your own time – you want time freedom. It's not really about the money but what that money can buy you. Everyone we have ever had on our courses always hates their job – doctors, teachers, business owners, social workers... They are not living their life on their terms. It's always the terms of their employment contract.

SUMMARY

Are you ready to go get your financial freedom? Is property a good investment? Our answer is unequivocally YES! Property can replace your income and provide you with a scalable business model for the rest of your life. It can give you financial reward and therefore freedom. However, it's not all sunshine and roses – you need to work hard now in order to enjoy the benefits later. And, most importantly, you need to start viewing lots of properties and making the commitment to it if you want to achieve these goals.

And there it is. Your roadmap to replacing your income with property. If you're excited by the prospect of replacing your income and becoming financially free, then we have great news for you. Property can be that vehicle! Not only can property provide a regular monthly income, but it can also be scaled up to provide a lifetime of wealth if you buy the right properties in the right locations.

Just start...

Never give up...

And just do one more thing...

We'd love you to join our New Era Property Training family. We all look out for each other and have some fun, but most importantly, come and share your journey with us and become your very own property millionaire.

To your future success!

FURTHER INFORMATION/ RESOURCES

To accompany this book are the Workbook and Property Millionaire Method Planner.

This is a working tool, to sit on your desk and hold you to account, but it also helps you to stay on track and follow the process. With lots of worksheets, pro-formas, you will have one place to collect all your property-investing thoughts and ideas. It's the essential tool for the serious millionaire property investor.

We have also put together a mini-course of materials to accompany the planner.

The planner can be obtained here: www.newerapropertytraining.co.uk/planner

Not only will the planner help you to take that daily action, but it will also become the difference between putting this book on the shelf, never to be started, and just doing one thing every day and finding yourself a property millionaire one day in the future.

THE AUTHORS

If you want to get into property and grow a million-pound portfolio, then you need to learn how to scale a property portfolio, and it's best to follow someone who has done that.

Briefly we, Rick and Lorraine Gannon, have grown an £8 million portfolio since 1997, much of which has been acquired in the last eight years. We had four properties for a long time. We flipped properties for profit, for many years. Renovated our own homes. It wasn't until we fine-tuned the Property Millionaire Method that we took off and saw massive growth in our personal wealth and incomes.

During the next two years we will double our current portfolio, and we plan to add 10 million pounds' worth of property. Remember we said earlier that you partner with time when investing in property, and effectively the longer you are in the property-investing market, the more it snowballs, and you grow faster and faster? With compounded growth, the opportunity to treble and quadruple our portfolio in a few short years is now very real.

We are effectively retired and don't have to work, but we choose to. While we have health, we envisage 'doing' something for a long time. Our children are still in full-time education and while we are supporting them, we must find something to do! Property is a perfect way of controlling your time but still having a focus and something to work towards.

We believe the human spirit is driven to do something meaningful, that when we don't grow or move forward as individuals, we are declining or decaying in some other way. Perhaps, when our children have flown the nest, we may go travelling.

For now, we invest in property. We invest in England and Wales.

Rick is an ex-police officer, author, property mentor and property management software tech founder (you can get a free 28-day trial of GoTenant at www.gotenant.co.uk).

Lorraine is a qualified business performance accountant with a background in turning around loss-making businesses so they can achieve high profits. She is also an author. Lorraine loves to use creative finance to buy property portfolios and do large deals, using the principal method described in this book.

So why set up a property training company, you might ask. We are glad you asked. Our training company is called New Era Property because we really believe that there is a 'new era' for the property market, property investors and tenants.

THE NEW ERA PROPERTY TRAINING VISION

New Era Training pledges to address the UK housing crisis in partnership with the private rental sector to innovate, reuse, repurpose and reconfigure property for residential multi-households. The UK needs 340,000 new homes annually just to keep up with the demand, but due to supply issues it has an annual shortfall of approximately 100,000 homes. The New Era vision is to create over 100,000 units of accommodation by training, guiding and developing 1,000 new property investors who each operate over 100 units of multi-let or single-let properties.

BACKGROUND TO THE NEW ERA VISION

We have run businesses for decades that are based on family values and community. We ran a chain of hotels, public houses and restaurants, employing over 85 people, for a decade. This team of people created spaces for families and friends to come together, they provided hospitality and formed communities. As a result, new families and lifetime friendships were formed.

Eventually, we decided to sell these businesses and Rick fulfilled a lifetime ambition of becoming a police officer. However, because Lorraine was working office hours as an accountant, our family lives started to suffer due to the shift work of the police; we were each working at different times. Realising something needed to change, we started to pick up our part-time property business and make this our full-time business.

Shortly after we left our jobs and became full-time property investors, working harder than ever to create a future for our family, we replaced our incomes for life. The life-changing effects of property have resulted in a better future for our family, more income and a legacy for our children. We could have stopped there, but with young children needing to be in school, the dream of retiring, doing nothing and living one long holiday becomes boring and unfulfilling when you realise you can't sit on a beach or in a Spanish bar all day, every day.

Of course, there is a middle ground, where we now spend almost all of the school holidays travelling, typically on a cruise ship or at our beach house in Wales.

Continuing to buy property and create family homes, we realised that New Era was creating homes and communities and helping with the housing shortage crisis. The New Era business was contributing already, but we asked ourselves 'how do we do more?'.

SUPPORTING UK HOMELESSNESS

The UK currently lacks the infrastructure to supply the new houses needed annually. Homelessness is increasing, with a huge gap of affordable housing.

We realised that even with a large portfolio of hundreds of tenants, our impact on the 100,000 new homes needed was insignificant. To solve the challenge of how to create over 100,000 new homes annually, we embarked on a vision to train others who could support and fill the gap. So New Era Property Training was created, and we decided to focus on assisting the private rental sector to innovate, reuse, repurpose and reconfigure property for residential multi-households. New property investors and new trainees can help alleviate the housing crisis all while finding passive income, growing personal wealth and supporting themselves and their family. Property can be win-win: it can help the homeless and support you and your lifestyle.

The New Era vision is to create over 100,000 units of accommodation by training, guiding and developing 1,000 new property investors who each operate over 100 units of multi-let or single let properties. This could be 16 multi-let properties or 100 single lets. It is a very challenging goal.

Through the students who engage and strive to realise the New Era vision, the New Era extended family was born. If you join our training programmes you will be asked to sign the New Era Vision & Pledge to support the cause.

SUPPORTING WORLD HOMELESSNESS

In 2015, the United Nations created 17 Sustainable Development Goals and aimed to achieve them by 2030. All 193 UN member states agreed on these 17 goals to end poverty, ensure prosperity and protect the planet.

United Nations Sustainable Development Goal 11: Make cities and human settlements inclusive, safe, resilient, and sustainable. By 2030, ensure access for all to adequate, safe and affordable housing and basic services and upgrade slums.

The right to housing is recognised in the Universal Declaration of Human Rights and yet over 20% of the world population – 1.6 billion people – still have inadequate access to housing. New Era also supports projects that go some way towards providing shelter to the many people in need across the world.

The UN goals address our wider aspiration to use profits and income to have impacts elsewhere in the world.

New Era donates to homelessness charities in India and Africa.

New Era is sponsoring projects in India by purchasing bricks for new homes to be built to support their vision that 'Every family deserves a decent place to live.'

If you enrol on an accelerator with us, we will donate 500 bricks to build a new home and pull a family out of slum conditions.

THE NEW ERA FAMILY

We are passionate about creating an impact on family issues, particularly those affecting children. Rick and Lorraine went to Buckingham Palace with the Duchess of Wessex in her capacity as President of Brainwaves Children's Charity in recognition of our charity work in raising funds for brain-damaged children. We also give to charities that provide mattresses to sick or disadvantaged children in India who would otherwise sleep on the floor while recovering. It is our aim to provide 1,000 mattresses, and we ask students to support this cause when enrolling on our courses.

As entrepreneurs we are always looking for ways to solve problems. Businesses solve problems, but it's not always about personal gain – we want to help others, by solving their problems too.

'Education is the most powerful weapon you can use to change the world.' - Nelson Mandela

---

Welcome to the New Era family.

ACKNOWLEDGEMENTS

Thank you to all our students who have helped us shape this method. Everyone who has been one of our students up to now has helped us to be better teachers and mentors. The privilege is all ours, to teach and mentor and see others get the same and better results. The distinctions and the subtleties you get when you understand a subject to a very deep and detailed level help you identify and spot trends and patterns. As your teachers and mentors, the lightbulb moments are accelerated, as we observe your results. Therefore, our students in return help us to keep developing and improving. Just as it should be. We thank you.

REFERENCES

[1] Credit Suisse Research Institute (2022). Global Wealth Report 2022. https://www.credit-suisse.com/media/assets/corporate/docs/about-us/research/publications/global-wealth-report-2022-en.pdf

[2] MacroTrends (2022). UK Life Expectancy 1950–2022. https://www.macrotrends.net/countries/GBR/united-kingdom/life-expectancy

[3] Halifax (2022). Halifax House Price Index, October 2022. https://www.halifax.co.uk/assets/pdf/october-2022-halifax-house-price-index.pdf

[4] Abraham H Maslow (1943). A Theory of Human Motivation. Psychological Review, 50(4), 370–396.

[5] White, A. The number of Londoners moving house more than doubled in 2021 – where did they go? Evening Standard (15 November 2021). https://www.standard.co.uk/homesandproperty/property-news/londoners-home-moves-house-prices-2021-b965902.html

[6] Trackcapital.co.uk

[7] Worldometer. Current World Population. https://www.worldometers.info/world-population/

[8] Edward O Wilson (2003) The Future of Life. London. UK: Little, Brown.

[9] Bramley, G (2019). Housing supply requirements across Great Britain for low-income households and homeless people: Research for Crisis and the National Housing Federation; Main Technical Report. https://researchportal.hw.ac.uk/en/publications/housing-supply-requirements-across-great-britain-for-low-income-h

[10] UK Parliament (2022). Research Briefing: Tackling the under-supply of housing in England. https://commonslibrary.parliament.uk/research-briefings/cbp-7671/

[11] HM Land Registry (2021). Press release: UK House Price Index for May 2021. https://www.gov.uk/government/news/uk-house-price-index-for-may-2021

[12] HM Land Registry. About Us. https://www.gov.uk/government/organisations/land-registry/about

[13] UK Health and Safety Executive. Maximum Penalties for Section 33 HSWA Offences. https://www.hse.gov.uk/enforce/enforcementguide/court/sentencing-penalties.htm#P1_32

[14] Office for National Statistics (2022). Index of Private Housing Rental Prices, UK: October 2022. https://www.ons.gov.uk/economy/inflationandpriceindices/bulletins/indexofprivatehousingrentalprices/october2022

[15] Office for National Statistics (2021). UK House Price Index: November 2021. https://www.ons.gov.uk/economy/inflationandpriceindices/bulletins/housepriceindex/november

[16] Bank of England. Official Bank Rate History. https://www.bankofengland.co.uk/boeapps/database/Bank-Rate.asp

[17] Marketing Sherpa (2012). The Complex Sale: Lead Scoring Effort Increases Conversion 79%. https://www.marketingsherpa.com/article/case-study/lead-scoring-effort-increases-conversion

[18] InsideSales.com

[19] Halifax (2022). Halifax House Price Index, October 2022. https://www.halifax.co.uk/assets/pdf/october-2022-halifax-house-price-index.pdf

[20] The Equality Trust. The Scale of Economic Inequality in the UK. https://equalitytrust.org.uk/scale-economic-inequality-uk